Spirit Communication

Connecting with Spirit Guides, Ancestors, Archangels, and Angels, along with Developing Your Psychic Mediumship Abilities Such as Channeling and Clairvoyance

Your Free Gift
(only available for a limited time)

Thanks for getting this book! If you want to learn more about various spirituality topics, then join Mari Silva's community and get a free guided meditation MP3 for awakening your third eye. This guided meditation mp3 is designed to open and strengthen ones third eye so you can experience a higher state of consciousness. Simply visit the link below the image to get started.

https://spiritualityspot.com/meditation

Table of Contents

Introduction

So you want to connect with the beings beyond this world. You want to know how to receive knowledge from them so you can live a better life, figure out the things that leave you confused, and learn about your true purpose in life. You'd like to know that no matter where you are, you're never alone and can always reach out to get help from the unseen world. This is the best book to help you with those goals.

You may have decided that you'd like to reach out to the spirit of someone near and dear to you who has passed on. Maybe you just feel a presence around you, and you've decided that you'd like to connect with it and see what it's about. No matter your reason for connecting with spirits, you'll find this book full of excellent material to help you make it possible. As you dive into the contents of this book, don't be surprised if you begin to pick up on spiritual energies. Also, expect the unexpected in a good way.

This book will give you all the information you need in clear English. Every concept is explained clearly, and you'll have practical, down-to-earth, straightforward, and easy-to-read knowledge that you can act on. You're going to find exercises and methods you can use to get in touch with the spirits who are all around you. You'll also learn how to stay safe as you reach out to the other side while discovering that *there is nothing for you to be afraid of.*

The best thing about this book is that you will find the information provided is not the average stuff you get from page one of a Google search. You'll dive deep into the world of spirits and discover how reaching out to them will give you a richer, more rewarding life. It doesn't matter what religious beliefs you hold or if you're not into religion *at all*. You'll find that spirits do not discriminate against others as humans do. The information in the pages of this book is so good that you'll find you don't have to be a monk or a priest to be able to sense and connect with the spirits that hover around all day, every day. The information works because it's not about external, performative religion but about spirituality, which is the realization that there's much more to life than that which can be observed with our physical senses.

Whether you desire to gain valuable information or to experience spiritual growth, you'll find that there is no better way than to reach out to those who know far more than we could ever hope to - the spirits around us, all day, every day. You must understand that you must keep an open mind and temporarily suspend your disbelief. You don't have to let others know that this is what you're doing. As you use the information from this book, keeping an open mind will bring you phenomenal results. Let's get started if you're ready to explore the minds of those beyond this world.

Chapter 1: Can We Really Communicate with the Spirits?

Since the dawn of time, people have tried to reach out to the dead and other entities beyond this realm. Though every human body will eventually die, the spirit that powers it will continue to live on, and they have interests in the life they lived when they were human. Most people are aware of this on some level, and some are more than simply aware. These people go on to make attempts to connect with the spirits which have transitioned from this life, hoping to remain in touch with them or gain information from them.

Spirits are a consciousness that has transitioned from this world but is still alive.
https://www.pexels.com/photo/mediums-sitting-in-circle-holding-hands-7267688/

Think about the number of times you've thought about calling someone, only to do so and find out they're going through something at that moment. You can pick up on that because you share ties with that person, and those ties make it possible to communicate with others physically and spiritually, too. These ties provide a connection that supersedes the physical world and its rules about how communication happens. This bond is often emotional, and it goes beyond life and death. Those who wish to reach out to spirits may want to reach out to their loved ones who aren't with them anymore. Spirits often try to reach out to us because they'd love to connect, too, whether to protect their loved ones, provide for them, comfort them, or just to say "Hi." The truth about life is that it goes on forever. Death is not the end, but a transition, which means it doesn't exist in the way we often think.

What Are Spirits?

What are spirits? Knowing how to define them will provide the framework you can use to reach out to them. Merriam-Webster defines a spirit as *"An animating or vital principle held to give life to physical organisms," "a supernatural being or essence," "the immaterial intelligence of the sentient part of a person," "the activating or essential principle influencing a person," or "the feeling, quality, or disposition characterizing something."*

When we talk about a spirit, we're talking about a consciousness that has transitioned from this world but is still alive. Additionally, it's a consciousness that can access the physical world and manipulate it in ways we can't see or understand, sometimes because even they do not understand it themselves. Because of this, many who work with spirits find it easier to think of them as "energy" rather than actual people because, in some ways, they think of them as being psychic projections of the dead.

Some spirits will remain on Earth because they don't realize that they're dead, while others will stick around because they want to be close to their loved ones or perhaps do some haunting. Some spirits can be benevolent and protective, while others are more malicious and dangerous. The reasons they behave in the way they do vary from spirit to spirit, but one thing remains constant. We must learn to listen and communicate with them to understand them better, which can ultimately lead us to a better understanding of death itself.

Some people hear the word spirit and immediately think about Casper, the friendly ghost, or something like that. Others think of a barely visible image that tends to hover just outside the realms of our ordinary five senses. While this is closer to the truth, that's not the whole picture. Everywhere, there are spirits. You've likely got a few around you right now. Some people are so gifted they can touch, hear, and see the spirits very clearly. Sometimes, you may spot a spirit from the corner of your eye when you're not looking right at it.

Types of Spirits

While many are scared of spirits, most of them are harmless. The only reason hauntings are considered scary is because of how they've been framed. Hauntings are simply situations where a spirit being is stuck in this realm because they have some unfinished business to handle. That said, you should note that not all spirits are human spirits. Knowing who and what you're connecting with is important to be safe and make the most of your interactions with these otherworldly beings is important. There are many kinds of spirits and other spiritual beings like entities. Let's take a look at each kind:

Ancestral spirits are your ancestors' spirits. These spirits will stick around because of the connection you share by blood. Sometimes you may have an ancestral spirit you met in person during their lifetime, and at other times you'll have ancestral spirits you never knew because they're from many generations before. You'll notice that ancestral spirits love nothing more than hanging around with family and are eager to connect with you so you can work together. They're lovely spirits to reach out to if you're just starting your spiritual path. This is because they're generally safe, and they'll keep you out of trouble.

Some spirits could cause you harm, but your ancestors usually have your back. It's not easy to have clear, proper boundaries when you're a newbie at spiritual work, so you should choose to work with your ancestors first, before any other kind of spirit. You may reach out to them and ask if they'd be interested in connecting with you and working together. Ancestral spirits can help you with your craft if you're a witch, as they can boost your powers and spells. They'll always be there to give you their assistance, and since you're their blood, you can expect that your spells will be powerful when you invoke them. Ancestral spirits will come to you in a way you can't miss. Don't be surprised if they appear in your dreams, looking much younger than the last time you met them while they were alive (if you did).

Earthbound spirits are like ancestral spirits in that they once lived on the earth. Mostly, they're here because they're still energetically connected to something that happened on earth or to a specific spot. They're the ones behind the harmless hauntings you know about. They often wind up here because they're stuck, and if their death was traumatic, they might just decide to remain around the death scene because it's not easy for them to let go of the hurt and pain inside. At other times, they stick around because they have some business they have to handle. Some spirits have passed on but don't realize their time on Earth is over, so they just hang around. They'll need a medium's help to set them free. Note that some spirits aren't stuck but simply want to pay Earth a visit.

Some spirits are considered scary, but in reality, they're the tormented spirits that are still bound to Earth and may not even know that they're being a menace to anyone. So you should have that in the back of your mind if you ever have any reason to deal with one.

Dead spirits are the same as ancestral spirits, but they're not connected to your bloodline. There are specific people that spirits of the dead like to hang around. For instance, the spirit of her deceased father may haunt a woman just because he wants to say hello, keep her safe, or provide for her. These spirits may also be earthbound. Sometimes they're not, meaning they can show up now and then just to keep track of what's happening here. For the most part, the spirits of the dead aren't dangerous. They just happen to know who you are and want to reach out.

If you notice a malevolent spirit, remember that you may be witnessing an earthbound spirit dealing with its trauma or a recording (more on that later). For the most part, spirits who hurt others are only doing so because they're in pain and unaware of it. Since there are good and bad people, it stands to reason that some spirits will have malicious intent. In this case, you need to realize that you have more power than they do on this plain, which means they have to use a lot of energy to move things around, even if you could move things easily.

If you're troubled by a spirit, you must do a cleansing, and you'll be just fine.

Spirit guides are meant to help you. They tend to be around you and are willing to give you all the guidance and advice you need. Your spirit guide could be an ancestral spirit, souls you have never known, angels, or ascended masters. Everyone has several guides assigned to them once they're born, and these guides can be changed to suit the phase of the person's life. You can also be specific about reaching out to a guide to help you with money.

Some witchcraft practitioners believe that you can have both negative and positive spirit guides, and both are necessary depending on what you want to accomplish. However, it would be best if you decided to focus on only getting the spirit guides who are good for your highest purpose and the best version of your life, which is yet to come.

Plant spirits are the spirits that are connected to the plants around you. You have to recognize that these spirits are real if you work with them, so if you aren't connected to them, the odds are you're just interacting with the physical aspect of the plant and not the spiritual side of it, which would be pointless. Plant spirits are safe, and their energy is gentle. As you become more aware of plant spirits, you'll find that each has its personality, needs, and desires. The best ones to interact with are the ones in your home or space, so you can be exposed to them enough to develop rapport with the plants. You may speak to them like their spirits are listening because they are. When you begin speaking with them, you activate them spiritually. So, take time to ask them if they'd like some more water, better placement in the sun, and so on. Pay attention to whether its spirit is outgoing or calm and gentle. If you don't have psychic abilities, this may be hard, but you can work with your intuition by choosing to trust it.

Mineral spirits aren't really common. Admittedly, they're not the rock stars of the spirit group, but you'll find they're everywhere. If you have stones, minerals, and crystals around you, the odds are you have mineral spirits with you. There are many of these spirits, as many as there are crystals and stones. You can reach out to them with your intuition, among other tools which will be covered later in this book.

Mineral spirits are interested in working with you on various aspects of your life. For instance, a mineral spirit may have relationships as its specialty, while another may be good for your mental health. These spirits love to connect with living humans, but for them, it is important that they are respected. So, you could ask them what they need so you can provide them. Note that certain spirits may not be interested in working with each other. When that happens, they're not pleased about having been sprung free from the Earth. In this case, you need to put the mineral back where you found it or somewhere which resembles it.

Negative entities are bad news, and you should avoid them at all costs by not seeking them out in the first place. These are parasitic beings, sucking all the energy they can get from you. These entities are not human. Some entities will latch on to you to get an energy boost before they take off. Other entities stick to you for a long time, feeding on your energy. When you notice you have these entities, you'll also find you feel depressed, angry, confused, and empty. There are many forms of negative entities, but they all have one thing in common. They are energy thieves that stubbornly latch on to you, refusing to let go. These are some of the most common ones:

- Energy vampires
- Black spirals
- Geopathic entities
- Henchmen
- Demons
- Negative ETs
- Disincarnates
- Witches or Warlocks
- Poltergeists
- Grays

Some of these entities exist as actual beings. The others play out as build-ups of energy with no sense of consciousness. Note that meditation, visualization, and other tools can eliminate negative entities. That said, knowing when these entities connect themselves to you is for the best. They'll come for you when you're doing something low-vibrational, and they're also drawn to you when you're with people with negative entities around them. You might also notice that when you're going through something traumatizing, a toxic relationship, or a difficult situation, you'll likely have entities wanting to hang out with you. They don't do physical damage, and you may be unaware of their presence, but they'll always affect your mind and energy, and soon enough, you'll be out of both if you don't cleanse yourself of them.

Goetic demons aren't actually demonic and can be helpful if you want to work with them. In fact, most witches are happy to have their assistance. The Lesser Key of Solomon talks about 72 of them. Each one has a specific skill. For instance, one is great with love, another with money, and so on. Note that these beings aren't the spirits of actual people, but instead, they are made up of the energetic signatures of different beings. Usually, they will help you with spells, but they want you to give them something. This means that you must beware of how you negotiate with them before giving them what they want.

Once more, these Goetic demons don't cause trouble unless and until you've summoned them. If you've got problems with a spirit, note that the Goetic demons are most likely blameless in the whole thing.

The Fae are spirits in another dimension not far from our own realm, which means you can physically reach out to them. It's easier to connect with the Fae than with other forms of spirits. Many shy away from seeking the Fae's assistance, but they can be helpful. For the most part, they are bound to specific locations. If you find one along your path, the odds are the spirit won't follow you back home unless your home is actually at the same location. The Otherworld is the world of the Fae, and there are various kinds of Fae you could work with. Working with them is safe as long as you do your homework first. Just because a being is spiritual doesn't mean they automatically owe you help. The Fae are like people too. There are good ones and bad ones, and shades of gray. You can't keep them away from your home if you upset them.

Elementals are the spirits that animate the elements of fire, air, water, and earth. They're meant to help protect nature and their element. Every tree has its own spirit, and the same goes for every body of water. The odds are you've got elemental spirits outside your home right now. Some traditions state that each element has proper gods and guardians. Some spirits are also meant to take care of specific aspects of nature. For instance, the Gnomes of the Fae kingdom are earth elementals. Salamanders are fire elementals, while undines are water elementals. Air elementals are called sylphs. When working with certain elements, ask for the help of the associated elemental.

Deities are the gods and goddesses of every religion and tradition who dwell in other realms. They can work with you depending on things like which religion you resonate with and so on. Before working with deities, you'll need to research them to know which ones you resonate with. You should also ensure that you're prepared for their energy as they're really powerful, and whatever you experience will be entirely up to them. This is why you need to dive deeply into each deity you'd like to work with before you invite them into your life. Another good way to choose a deity is to set the intention that you want to work with the best deity for you and your goals and then keep your eyes peeled so you can see the signs that tell you who your deity is. You should make offerings to them regularly to keep your connection strong when you do come to know the entity.

Angels are the spirits that many people work with. Many types of myths surround these wonderful beings, and they have much more knowledge than most other beings, such as ancestral or dead spirits. The power and might of an angel should not be underestimated. In fact, you may never be able to fully comprehend the extent of their power. The thing about angels is that they think in black and white and are particular about what they consider good or bad. Research their mythology before you work with them, and learn about how they're viewed through different religions and cultures.

Demons are the last on this list, and they've always seemed scary when they're really not. Where angels are organized, demons aren't. An angel has a specific task, while a demon doesn't. Also, you should note that a demon's chaotic energy doesn't mean it's an evil entity. It just means that it's hard to predict what will come next when you work with them. There are other demons besides the Goetic ones. If you're a chaos witch, you'll want to work with demons since there's power in the chaos. Note that these beings aren't evil and are not good either. They have no bias and can bend either way. Some of them love to work with humans, but at a cost, of course. You need to be sure of what you're negotiating with them so that you're both okay with the final agreement. Note that there are demons that can be bad and terrifying, but this doesn't mean they're all like that. In fact, the Fae, angels, some ancestors, and other kinds of spirits can be scary, too. So ensure that you're protected when you work with them and be clear about what you desire before you call upon a demon.

The odds are a demon won't come to you if you don't reach out to them, so if you sense some negative being in your home and you haven't summoned them, you may be dealing with something else. Generally speaking, it's much more sensible to be careful with other entities rather than with demons. However, that doesn't mean that you should ignore just how powerful these beings are. Some of them can also exert physical power and move large things to hurt you. It's best not to summon them because they're not easy to get rid of when you've finished working with them, so you need to be good about cleansing your space and warding them off. You should also know how to work with banishing spells before you call the demons, so you can eliminate them if needed. This is a good thing to do unless you're dealing with other kinds of spirits who are loving and kind.

A Brief History of Spiritual Communication

Spiritualism became a religion that took the world by storm, and communicating with spirits through mediumship was popular in the United Kingdom and the United States. Mediumship begins with the Witch of Endor's story. The witch of Endor was also a medium who had brought the spirit of a dead prophet named Samuel back to life so that Saul, the Hebrew king, could ask him some questions. Around the early '80s, some scientists looked into Spiritualism and soon converted. While some frauds used magic tricks to make people believe they were in touch with spirits, there were some genuine mediums.

Spirit Communication Today

A study by Julie Beiscel and Gary E Schwartz demonstrated that some mediums can get accurate information about those who have passed on. Another study with at least 1,000 participants over eight years found that some humans can predict the future. The results of this study were published in the paper Feeling the future: Experimental evidence for anomalous retroactive influences on cognition and affect" by Daryl Bem in 2011.

Frequently Asked Questions

What is spirit communication?

Spirit communication is also known as mediumship. It is the spiritual practice of communicating with the spirit world. Practitioners are known as mediums, and they use tools such as tarot cards, pendulums, and often writing to perform readings from spirits that have crossed over into the living world in physical or non-physical forms, as well as other spirit beings. Mediums typically receive messages about what spiritual lessons we should take away from these past lives to help us grow spiritually in this life and prepare for our next existence. Mediums also assist spirits in preparing to pass on, so they may move on to a better place.

Where do spirits go after death?

Spirits continue to exist and evolve after the death of their bodies. Many move into a non-physical or spiritual realm called heaven or the spirit world. A medium often speaks with spirits who have passed over to this world from ours. Sometimes they remain in the astral world that overlaps ours, which is why we may dream about them or sense their presence sometimes, even if we can't see them.

What does the afterlife look like?

There are many different ideas about what the afterlife looks like. Many believe that it is a place of peace, happiness, and learning for those who have passed over, and it may be an eternal return to the world we knew before or one where we create something entirely new. The afterlife could also simply be the next phase of life in the soul's evolution that has moved on. In other words, it's their next incarnation.

Can anyone talk to spirits?

Yes. Anyone can learn how to do mediumship. It is a skill you can learn, and you don't have to be "gifted" to do it. You need to learn the techniques and access your innate mediumistic abilities.

How long does it take to learn mediumship?

It all depends on how much you want to learn and how much time you want to devote to it. There are many different ways to learn and practice this skill, so it is not like riding a bike. So, choose the right path if you want to learn the art of mediumship and how to connect with the spirit world. Just select the tool that you can relate to the most.

How do I become a medium?

You can learn mediumship by attending classes or groups, reading books, and practicing independently. There are many ways to practice and learn to communicate with people's spirits. Many people learn intuitively or through visits from spirit guides in dreams or visions. The idea is to open up your mind and heart to the possibilities of the afterlife, so you can communicate with those who have passed over. Reading this book is a great start.

Will I get in trouble for contacting spirits?

No, you are not breaking any laws by contacting spirits. Most people open themselves up to mediumship to connect with their loved ones who have passed on. There's nothing wrong with that.

Is communicating with spirits safe?

Yes, it is safe and a very positive experience. It can be a way to establish a line of communication with the spirit world. In some cases, spirits may also use mediums as messengers for those who have passed on, which can be very rewarding.

Chapter 2: Tapping into Your Psychic Abilities

We live in a day and age where many of us seek guidance. Whether it be about managing careers, relationships, illnesses, or simply how to live our lives more intentionally, finding answers from traditional sources can lead you on a long winding journey of frustration and uncertainty. We have turned away from religion, lost faith in government officials and doctors, and relied on science for all the answers. But what if there was something else? What if you could contact those who hold the answers in the spirit realm? What if they could give you clear answers, guidance, and direction? You can get all that and more if you want. All you need to do is work with your psychic senses. There are four psychic abilities known as the four clairs. These are:

Clairvoyance refers to the ability to "see clearly."
https://www.pexels.com/photo/a-woman-holding-a-locket-7278743/

- Clairvoyance
- Clairaudience
- Clairsentience
- Claircognizance

Every clair is considered extra sensory perception, or ESP, because they're supposed to be extensions of our five senses. Some psychics and occultists have different ideas. They believe that the physical senses aren't the root of the extrasensory senses but are instead a physical manifestation that comes from the psychic senses. It's not easy to prove this theory, but it does line up with a post-materialist perspective, which holds that everything springs from consciousness, and without consciousness, nothing would exist. Note that other clairs exist besides these four, but these are the most common ones.

Clairvoyance

Clairvoyance is a term that is sometimes used to refer to every psychic ability under the sun, but it really refers to the ability to "see clearly." It is the ability to perceive events and images at a distance and through time. Sometimes, it's considered an extension of regular eyesight.

In light of the view that all things come from consciousness, one could assume that means everyone is clairvoyant. Most people have their first taste of clairvoyance in childhood, while others come across this ability as grown-ups. All around you are subtle energies that you may not be aware of all the time, but that doesn't mean you don't interact with them. Those with very strong clairvoyance will likely perceive these energies easily, without training or effort. Generally speaking, the clairvoyant ability is accessible to one and all and may lie dormant in you. You can reactivate this ability. For instance, you can practice seeing and reading auras, subtle energies surrounding all living objects and beings.

Clairvoyance has a lot to do with all sorts of experiences that involve the extended abilities of sight. Also, there is inner clairvoyance and outer clairvoyance. The latter version of this ability lets you see the energies and spirits as an overlay over your physical space, as is the case with those who can see the physical manifestation of spirits. Think of it like augmented reality. External clairvoyance lets you see the spirits so clearly that they're as real as any other regular person around you. Sometimes, the beings are seen not as clear manifestations but as shadows that move, sparks of light, glowing orbs, and so on. The ability to perceive any realm besides the physical one and subtle energies using just the eyes is a form of external clairvoyance.

Then there's the matter of inner clairvoyance. Here, you see things with your mind's eye. It's almost like imagination, except you're not necessarily manipulating images you get as you may have if you were daydreaming. You see things on the viewing screen of your mind. Examples of inner clairvoyance include psychic dreams, remote viewing, precognition, and premonition.

Martin's story: "*I remember having strange visions from when I was four. When I was about seven, my mom and dad took me on a trip to visit some friends of theirs in Lagos, Nigeria. As soon as I walked into their yard, I looked at the house, and what I saw was inexplicable and frightening. The house was crumbling and caving in, and I kept wondering why my parents were trying to get me to enter. I kept saying, "The house is falling." and freaking out, but they calmed me down and took me in anyway, and as soon as I walked through the front door, everything seemed normal. We left two weeks later. I still remember my father being on the phone with his friend as he exclaimed, "No," My mother, curious, asked him what the matter was. It turned out their friends' home had collapsed a month later. Fortunately, they made it out okay. I've never forgotten that experience. After that, I remember thinking I don't want to see things before they happen anymore.*

Clairvoyance, or Just Imagining?

You need to be able to tell the difference between what you imagine versus what's an actual message from spirits through your clairvoyance. When you get images from spirits, you're not the one in charge of what you see. You can't bend or twist the information to show you something else. It will just flash in your mind's eye without you trying to make it happen. If you feel any force or effort on your part when you see images in your mind's eye, the odds are you're only imagining.

How to Develop Clairvoyance

Work with Your Visualization and Imagination More

Whenever you use your imagination, you awaken your clairvoyant ability. This is because your imagination or mind's eye is the medium through which you receive the images you get. The better you are at imagining, the easier it will be for you to develop your clairvoyance.

Visualize Your Third Eye

Imagine having a third eye that sits right above and between both eyes. You already do have a third eye, even though you may not be able to see it. In this visualization exercise, you'll imagine that this third eye is closed. Then, imagine the eyelid opening up slowly. This visualization exercise aims to help you bring your intention to your subconscious mind that you'd like to awaken your dormant clairvoyance. When you do this exercise regularly for at least five to ten minutes a day, you fuel your intention with energy, and this will cause your actual third eye to follow your lead.

Work with Crystals

You can go to bed with a lapis lazuli crystal or an amethyst beneath your pillow, with the intention that you'll awaken your psychic abilities. You can also place the crystal where your third eye is located so that it can awaken this inner vision that is yours. Note that there may be other crystals you're drawn to for this purpose, so you should simply follow whatever pulls you.

Begin with the Eyes Closed

When it comes to developing clairvoyance, you may find that inner clairvoyance is much easier to begin with than outer clairvoyance. So you should close your eyes for at least five to ten minutes a day and then state your intention out loud or quietly to yourself that you're open to seeing whatever the spirit you're working with thinks is important for you to see.

Use Affirmations

You can work with affirmations, like "I am extremely clairvoyant," to help you. To do this, you can just sit comfortably, close your eyes, and repeat this to yourself with conviction for at least ten to fifteen minutes. Your mind may argue with you, but this isn't the time to be reasonable or rational. Just trust that your words will dictate your experience. If you want even more powerful affirmations, you can phrase them as though they're already a thing of the past. In other words, you could affirm any of the following:

- How did I become so clairvoyant? (This is an "affirmation.")
- I remember when I wasn't clairvoyant. Now I see everything.
- It's amazing how much better I've become at clairvoyance.

You may work with these affirmations or phrase them however you see fit.

Practice Meditation Every Day

Something about the practice of sitting in silent observation of your breath for anywhere from five to fifteen minutes each day can powerfully awaken your dormant abilities. Make sure you wear something comfortable and are free from distractions. Ask not to be disturbed if you don't live alone. Then bring your attention to your breath as you close your eyes. Breathe in through your nostrils and out through slightly parted lips. As you do this, your attention will wander away from your breath. This is fine. Simply notice and bring your attention back to your breath as often as it happens, and never beat yourself up for getting distracted. The whole point of the exercise is to awaken you to the subtle energies around you, help you channel your attention where you want it to be, and open you up to the messages that spirits around you may have for you.

Clairaudience

Clairaudience is "clear hearing," which means it's about being able to hear spirits. Sometimes it's the little voice you hear inside you when you're about to do something or go somewhere you shouldn't or when you're being led to something that will help you tremendously in life. At other times, it's quite loud and clear, often freezing you in your tracks and not giving you the time or capacity to question it. This voice reaches out to you when you have to make an important decision that could alter your life for better or worse. If you're not naturally clairaudient, you can work on this. If you are, the odds are that most of your messages come to you from your Higher Self and other spirits through this means. You'll get messages through songs, words, sounds, and more. The messages could come from within or from without. You may also experience hearing the spirits as you go to bed, wake up, or dream.

Clairaudients naturally hear more than the average person. Those who don't like loud sounds are likely clairaudients, even though they may not be aware of it because they're more sensitive to sounds than others. Clairaudients also tend to experience ringing in the ears, and no, it's not tinnitus. They get this ringing or loud-pitched tone in their ears because spirits ask them to pay attention to the moment or tune in to their inner hearing and listen.

Some of the most clairaudient people are musicians or musically inclined. Many of them hear melodious songs within themselves, or they have dreams of melodies they know they could not have come up with before putting them on paper. If you want to develop this ability yourself, you need to begin working more consciously with your hearing so you can fine-tune it.

Charity's story: *"I had often wondered about my husband's behavior toward me in the days leading up to what I call "the end." I remember I couldn't put my finger on what was wrong, and talking to him wasn't resolving things. He wasn't doing anything I could point out was wrong, and I wondered for a while if I was being paranoid. Fed up with the feeling that way, I wanted the feeling to stop, so I reached out to my guide for help that night. The next day, while he was out at work and I was working at home, I heard a very clear message in my mind: "Go and log into the old laptop your husband abandoned two months ago." I grabbed the thing and fired it up. I never knew his password or asked, so I sat there staring at the screen, confused. Then I got a word: "Novia." I had never heard that word before but decided to type it in. I was flabbergasted by the fact that the password actually worked. This voice showed me many things I had no idea were happening under my roof. I found out that my husband had been cheating on me. He had been unfaithful to me for more than two years and had planned to leave me in a couple of months. I was finally free and happy.*

How to Develop Clairaudience

Pay Attention to the Sounds around You

When you go to bed each night, lie in the dark and pay attention to what you can hear. You should do this at night because it's easier to make it a habit when you attach it to something you have to do every day; you *can't get by without sleep*, so bedtime is a good time to practice this. Pay attention to every sound from near and far. Usually, when you need to focus on something or want to sleep, you'll tune out these sounds. You should start doing the opposite. As you do this, notice every sound that makes up the general noise you can hear. Some are more subtle than others. Practicing this for a week can give you mind-blowing results.

Keep Your Mind Attuned to Clairaudient Messages

All you have to do is visualize a radio. Turn it on. Assume that one of the stations you can get with that radio is your intuition, your ancestor spirits, or whatever else you may want to connect to. Envision yourself tuning in to that frequency. If you want, imagine this brings your spirit guides around a table with you, ready to answer any questions you may have. Notice if you're picking up on any message from them. Sometimes, the voices that come through will be very clear so that you know exactly what they're saying. Sometimes, hearing them may not be easy, or you may get nothing. If that's the case, that's not enough reason to give up. Continue this practice, and you'll find yourself doing better at picking up clairaudient messages.

Practice Meditation Daily

Like all other clairs, this ability can be honed by sitting in silence daily. Remember, you don't need more than fifteen minutes.

Use Affirmations

You can do this right after your meditation session so that you're in a receptive mode to the suggestions you're giving your subconscious mind. You can use the following affirmations:

- *I clearly hear what spirits have to say to me all the time*
- *I remember when I couldn't hear a thing from spirits. Now it's every day.*
- *My clairaudient ability is at its peak*
- *My inner ears are always open to what spirits have to say*

Other things that can help you develop this ability are:

1. Set a clear intention that you want to use this ability. Writing it down makes it more likely to happen.
2. Choose not to be afraid of whatever you hear, good or bad. Being afraid is a good way to block your clairaudience, as your

Higher Self isn't interested in spooking you unnecessarily.

3. Use binaural beats on the Internet to help you become more clairaudient.

Clairsentience

Clairsentience is "clear-feeling." This is a very grouped gift and one that is used by many people daily. It's basically letting your feelings guide you. For instance, you may feel off at the moment, and then you decide to step away from where you are on the curb, only for an accident to happen right where you were standing moments ago. Or you may feel weird and then turn around to find that it's because someone has been staring at you long and hard.

Clairsentient messages come to you through gut feelings, empathy, and physical sensations. When it comes to your gut feelings, those are strong emotions you get that you can almost feel physically in your body. Think of intense fear or excitement. You know your actions are right when you feel good in your gut. When you get sick, you know how to get out of your situation or stop dealing with something. If you paid more attention to your gut, you'd probably be in less trouble than you are now.

Empathy is what lets you know how others are feeling or what it's like to be them. It makes it easy to experience life as someone else – but if you're not careful, you may have trouble telling which emotions are yours and which aren't, especially if you're an empath. When it comes to clairsentience through physical sensations, you may notice a tingle along your spine, a shiver, a change in air pressure or temperature, or tickling. These are just some of the sensations you get as you connect with the spirits through clairsentience.

Lulu's story: *"It's a funny thing, but when I'm about to make a decision about something, I get really uncomfortable prickly sensations in my body when it's a bad decision, and when it's a good one, the top of my head feels like cool air's blowing on it. The one time I disregarded this and went ahead with something I was getting prickles about; it didn't work out. Lesson learned."*

How to Develop Clairsentience

Read Other People's Energies

Ask a good friend to get a picture of someone they know who you don't know at all. Look at the person's eyes in the picture to get a lock on their energy. Is it positive or negative? Ask yourself questions about this person, like what they're like as a person. Ask yourself if you can pick up anything from their eyes, and then let your friend know your findings. Your friend should let you know if you were spot on or not. Try this as often as possible until you get better at it.

Practice Psychometry

This is an exercise where you'll get an object that belongs to someone. It's got to be something the person has worn often, as the more you wear something, the more it absorbs your energy. As you develop your clairsentience, you should be able to read the residual energy from objects. Hold the item in your hands for a minute or more, and notice if you're picking up on positive or negative energy.

Pay Attention to Your Chakras

In this exercise, you'll connect with your own energy centers and read the energy you give off. You should learn about chakras first before you do this exercise. This is a good exercise because you'll learn more about how you feel and what emotions you embody every time you do this. Sit or lie in a comfortable position, and then begin with the first or root chakra. In your mind's eye, see it as a colored wheel or orb of light that spins, and let the light extend outside of your body by at least a few inches. Then check how you feel about the chakra, and notice what emotions come up. You may also notice certain sensations in your body that will let you know how you're really doing in life.

Claircognizance

Claircognizance is "clear-knowing." If you're claircognizant, you have a way of knowing things you shouldn't know without anyone telling you. You get the information in thought form from the spirits you interact with. Sometimes, it's just a thought, and at other times you get blocks of thoughts called "downloads" because it seems like they're downloaded into your mind. You may have inspired ideas about situations, people, and places. The claircognizant often strongly believes that what they know is true, even though they cannot logically say why. Often, the information they get turns out to be accurate.

Claircognizants tend to love working with their minds a lot. They're mentally talented people who love to analyze things and break them down in their minds. These people are excellent problem solvers and good at seeing the connections between things that others would miss. These people had an answer for everything, even when they were children, and were probably snubbed for being "know-it-alls." This ability isn't well-known, as more people know clairaudience and clairvoyance. Just because this power is subtle doesn't mean that it's not effective and powerful. Claircognizance can express itself through automatic writing and channeling, as well. You may get a truly amazing idea, or you somehow know how something will work out. You might get the sense that someone is being dishonest, or you know you should pass up an opportunity because something about it is off and not good for you. In those cases, you may have experienced claircognizance.

The difference between claircognizance and your thoughts is that your conscious mind cannot control your claircognizant messages. It can only witness the information. With claircognizance, if you trust your ability, the odds are you'll never question a claircognizant message. Also, your recurring thoughts are rooted in the ego, and the ego works to keep you safe from being disappointed, embarrassed, or from failing. Claircognizance is beyond the ego and is rooted in wisdom. It also demands that you act on the information based on faith.

Hailey's story: *"I've noticed that whenever I'm confused about something or it stresses me out, all I have to do is decide that the answers and solutions will come to me when they're ready and then forget about the problem. I'll get struck by an idea to handle the problem a certain way, and it's usually the right call. There have also been times when I was supposed to be part of something I've always wanted to participate in, only to wake up in the morning with a strong knowledge that I shouldn't leave my home. I usually end up seeing why following that knowledge was a good idea later on. Either I hear the event I was supposed to go to didn't happen, or I find out that there's something better and easier lined up for me.*

How to Develop Claircognizance

Practice automatic writing

This is a good way to improve your claircognizance. Get a piece of paper or start a new document on your computer. Tell the spirit you're working with that you'd like to reach out to them. You can ask them questions or let them speak to you about whatever they want. When you write, don't think. Just note whatever first comes into your mind, even if it seems gibberish or doesn't make sense initially. Don't judge it, don't question it, and have no expectations about what the message may be. Your conscious mind is only there to be a witness, not to control things. You may get nonsense the first few attempts, but after a while, some golden nuggets will begin to flow through you. With time and practice, you won't need to sit for too long before information begins to flow.

Set the Intention to Be More Claircognizant

Write your intention down somewhere you can see it. You can write it down first thing in the morning and the last thing at night, too.

Set Time Aside to Receive Messages from Your Intuition or Spirit

You can do this after meditation, so you'll have a mind more conducive to knowing what you need.

Work with Your Crown Chakra

This chakra is on top of your head. Imagine a vortex with white light that spins on top of your head. Feel it open up, using your imagination. Imagine a stream of light flowing in through that energy center. The stream of light is spiritual knowledge and wisdom. Then frame your questions in your mind, and sit and wait for the answers to come through. Practice this daily for the best results.

Chapter 3: Getting Ready for Spirit Work

You know the saying, "Proper preparation prevents poor performance." So, this chapter is dedicated to everything you need to know about how to prepare for your spiritual journey. You can't just decide to start working with spirits without laying the groundwork for success first – which means getting your mind, body, and spirit ready for the task ahead. If you don't take time to do the prep work, you may encounter difficulties along the way. For instance, you may have trouble establishing a clear connection with the spirit you want to reach. Even worse, you may attract the attention of spiritual beings you want to avoid at all costs. You may also find that each session you spend communicating with spirits tends to leave you drained and out of sorts. If that's the case, it can be difficult to enjoy the practice, let alone keep going with it, and you may miss out on all sorts of good things.

Before doing any spiritual work, you must ground yourself.
https://www.pexels.com/photo/women-holding-hands-at-a-table-with-burning-candles-7267684/

What Is Grounding?

Grounding connects you to the Earth's energy. What's the theory? It's believed that the Earth transmits reliable and grounded energy, a resource for dealing with difficult times. Who can ground themselves? Anyone can use grounding to eliminate negative energy in their body so they can feel better and be more open to the subtle energies of the spirit world. Also, it helps to get you in the right mindset for the work ahead of you.

Before doing any spiritual work, you must ground yourself because the spiritual mediumship and development process can raise your energy levels to unhealthy heights. And since you'll be helping spirits with their business, you don't want any energy-related illnesses like high blood pressure, headaches, or dizziness. Also, you don't want to create a situation where you're so carried away by the spiritual work that you no longer handle the mundane, day-to-day stuff that you should.

A Grounding Meditation

This is a meditation used to center your energy. If you have never meditated before, find a quiet space where you can relax and will not be interrupted. You may keep your eyes open or closed, but it is recommended that you keep them closed. You can lie on the ground, sit on it, or sit on a chair but make sure your feet are bare and firmly planted on the floor beneath you.

Lightly rest your hands on your stomach (or on the surface of your yoga mat or surface surrounding you). Remember that your intentions are the most important factor in this ritual, so if you want to feel lighter, more present, or more energetic, don't just focus on the breathing but the intention. Begin to breathe slowly in through your nostrils and out through your slightly parted lips.

Imagine a powerful red light coming up through the earth and into your body wherever it connects with the floor. Let this light either bring you the energy you need or take away what you don't need. For the former, see energy moving from the earth into your body. For the latter, see your body's chaotic energy in the form of black smoke moving into the earth to be absorbed by its red light. If you're not good at visualization, you can imagine the feeling of the energy flowing in the direction you want it to. Keep going until you feel focused and grounded.

Clearing Your Mind

Before doing spirit work, your mind has to be clear so you can focus on the only thing that matters; the intention you have for the work you're about to do. You can't escape your mind, so you should do your best to keep it clear and free because that's how you get the best results when working with spirits. The following are things you can do to clear your mind for the task ahead.

Write Down Your Feelings or Thoughts as They Come Up

Sometimes, we tend to change our minds so quickly that we don't even realize how mad or sad we can get until it's too late and we meditate in a bad mood. By writing it down before meditating, you can analyze your feelings, possibly discovering that they are not simply based on a current situation but something deeper.

Go for a Walk in Nature

One lovely thing to do is to go for a walk by the river. When you're out in nature, you can feel the spirits around you, and when you go for a walk by the river, trees, or in the sunlight, it just seems so much more like you're in your natural element. Nothing is better than getting fresh air and walking among trees and grass. There's also nothing that gives you more peace than feeling at one with nature while taking time out of your schedule to get away from society and just be with yourself.

Meditate on the Spiritual Aspect of the Problem

Sometimes, we get so wrapped up in the idea that we need to keep busy with our lives that we forget about spirituality. If you are feeling overwhelmed, then first ask yourself if your life is going according to what you set out to do or if there's something else you wanted to do that somehow fell off your schedule. If it isn't, ask yourself what it is you want and how you can live in a way that doesn't cause stress. If it is simply a matter of being too busy and not spending enough time with your family or friends or doing whatever activities are important to you due to obligations from school or work etc., then ask yourself, have you done everything that you can to make things work? And if the answer is no, then it's time to re-evaluate how your life is going.

Meditate to Help You Find What You Need

Sometimes, it's hard to have a clear mind if you're struggling with stress and other issues in life. Most people who want to meditate want to get rid of their stress. At least for the short term. But it's important to understand that meditation isn't about getting rid of anything. It's about finding out what you need. Stress is a result of unaddressed needs. The first step is usually coming to terms with your situation for the time being, but after that, you have to ask yourself what you need to do to find strength and grow as a person. Sometimes it is pretty clear, sometimes not. For example, if you feel like life is going too fast and you want a break from the craziness of your life, then go ahead and take one, but if you need to find something spiritually powerful inside yourself, try meditating on it. If this seems too hard a task, try meditating to notice how you feel, so you can release what doesn't serve you.

Don't Be Afraid to Ask for Help

Don't be afraid of finding a teacher who can show you techniques that can help you clear your mind if nothing you do is working for you. Ask for whatever you need from the universe to help you along the way, and do your best to put in an honest effort. As long as you're not doing everything for yourself and contorting your energy, spirits will come through with the right form of help for you.

Raising Your Vibration

There are many exercises to raise your vibration for spiritual work, including visualization, meditation, drumming, and dancing. Let's look at a few.

Meditation: This can be done by sitting on a cushion or sofa with your eyes closed. Focus on visualizing a white light in the center of your being – which expands outwards from you into the universe. It also helps to use an object as a focal point during meditation, such as a candle or crystal ball, as your meditative focal point.

Dancing and Drumming: In these types of practices, it is recommended that you incorporate movement to achieve higher levels of awareness and consciousness. There are many videos of shamanic drumming that you can find for free on the Internet to help you to raise your vibration.

Mantras: Mantras are a great way to connect with your higher self and help to raise your vibration. There are many different types of mantras, for example, the "peace be still" mantra "Om Shalom Shanti" or the "Om Mani Padme Hum," which means "Hail to the Jewel in the Lotus."

Sharing Intentions: This practice has been used by native people to reach people they may wish to get guidance from or perhaps even just let their loved ones know that they're thinking about them. This practice can be done practically anywhere at any time. Once you've set the intention, simply speak your intention out loud and feel it in your heart.

Tuning In: This practice is used when we need to tune in to our higher self or to help us become aware of the energy of others. It is also a good way to get us in touch with our collective consciousness, which can provide guidance and inspiration. This can be done by simply tuning in using intent and focusing on the energy of your Higher Self or any spirit you want to work with.

Visualization: Visualization is a powerful practice that can help you reach different levels of consciousness and awareness. It works by helping you to see your surroundings differently by creating imagery in your mind of what you want to achieve. This could be an image of yourself holding up an energy ball towards the universe, an image of the end result you want to get from interacting with the spirits, or a scene with your spiritual guides or loved ones. Once you have this image in mind, use your intention and focus on this vision until it becomes real for you.

Positive Affirmations: Having positive affirmations is just as important as having intentions. Positive affirmations are statements about our lives that we believe to be true or want to be true. They are mostly positive statements used to help you validate yourself and your spirituality by helping to raise your vibration. Some examples of these affirmations include: "I am a Light Being" or "I am already doing the work that I need to do to achieve my goals."

Occult Symbolism and Why It Matters

What exactly is the occult? The term "occult" comes from the Latin word *occultus*, which means hidden. It was originally a term for knowledge of the supernatural that was kept secret and only passed on through the generations from master to student. The source of this information could be magical-religious in nature or not. This encompassed subjects considered taboo, such as astrology, alchemy, magic, divination, and witchcraft.

It is believed that occult knowledge originated from prehistoric religions when it served as a bridge between man and God. The ancient pagan religions had their own set of rituals and symbols that related to different elements of nature, stars, the seasons, and the cycles of life. These symbols were used to convey specific messages from the spirit world to people to understand and interpret these messages as best as possible. The knowledge about them was passed on orally from one generation to another. Later, with the expansion of literacy, written records started appearing. This was when some occult practices became more widespread and common knowledge among different societies.

Many people are interested in spirituality and ritual work but don't know much about the occult. Having a basic knowledge of what's going on is not only interesting, but it's also important. By learning more about the occult and its symbols, you'll better understand what you're working with during your rituals. You don't need to know too much, just enough to use it for personal purposes. As you learn more about them, you will also understand why and how they're used for your personal spirit work. You'll also grasp the messages that the spirits are trying to share with you even better.

One-Week Prep for Spirit Work

The following is a seven-day preparation routine to help you begin your spiritual work. When you wake up each morning or when you go to bed at night:

1. **Ground Yourself**: You're just waking up and want to be fully present. You can just sit up in bed with your feet on the floor for five minutes while you breathe consciously. Grounding yourself at the end of the day is okay, so you can shed the energetic debris of the day.

2. **Meditate:** When you've finished grounding yourself, it's time to meditate. Do this for at least five minutes and, at most, ten minutes. You can get right into the meditation from the grounding process. This will help clear your mind and get you

in the headspace needed to receive psychic communication.

3. **Visualize Your Chakras Opening Up:** If you're not good at visualizing, imagine the sensation of more energy flowing through each chakra, from the root to the crown.

4. **Affirmations:** Affirm to yourself that you're now sensitive to every good spiritual being with nothing but the best of intentions and your highest good in mind. Phrase this affirmation however you like. Don't be surprised if you begin sensing the presence around you.

5. **Fast Forward:** Now, mentally move yourself to a time in the future when you're very adept at communicating with spirits. Imagine that you just finished a session with them, and thank them. Feel deep appreciation in your heart for the clarity of their messages. Do this for five minutes.

If you don't want to do these steps all at once, you can split them however you like, so you do some when you wake up and the others when you go to bed. Do this consistently for seven days, and you'll see phenomenal results.

Chapter 4: Channeling the Spirits

Now that you've gone through the preparatory week, you're ready to start working with the spiritual realm and its inhabitants. Ideally, you should wait until you have finished reading the book before you begin your practice, especially the last chapter, which has some pertinent information you must have if you want to practice spirit work safely and powerfully. You must know how to cleanse yourself before and after work to avoid issues.

It's a known fact that the best way to dive deep into the truth of our existence is to enter into a trance state.

https://www.pexels.com/photo/a-woman-sitting-at-the-table-7278733/

In this chapter, you'll learn about getting into a trance state, the steps to enter a trance, and how you can transmit your questions and intentions to the spirits you're working with. You'll also learn the importance of closing the connection when you've finished and how to do that. Before getting into all this information, please beware of deliberately seeking out negative entities with malicious intentions. Ideally, you should have friendly spirits like your ancestors around you when you work with other spirits so that they can keep you safe in case there's any funny business from other spirits you're dealing with.

What Is a Trance State?

Going into a trance is an ancient practice. For several thousands of years, humans have used all sorts of methods to alter the state of their consciousness so they can connect with the worlds unseen. Many traditions, cultures, and religions incorporate trance states in their spiritual practices. It's a known fact that the best way to dive deep into the truth of our existence is to enter into a trance state. Regardless of your spiritual practices and beliefs, you'll find the trance state is very useful for deepening your spiritual journey. If you want to connect with spirits, you should definitely learn to get into a trance. The question is, what is that?

A trance state is a different state of mind or consciousness from your ordinary waking consciousness, which you're using to read this book. In this state, you're neither fully awake nor quite asleep. In other words, the trance state sits on the razor-thin edge between the conscious and subconscious minds. The trance state is what you achieve when you're off daydreaming or zoning out. You need to remember five levels when it comes to trance states.

Very Light Trance: This is level one. At this stage, your awareness moves to focus predominantly on what's happening inside you. At this point, you become aware of what you're thinking and how you feel physically and emotionally. If you practice meditation regularly, odds are you already know what it is like to enter this state of consciousness.

Light Trance: This is level two. You can tell you're at this level because the consciousness you experience will be akin to a dream. Think about how it feels to fantasize and get lost in worlds you created in your mind. This is what it feels like in this level of trance. If you're watching the television, reading a book, or taking a trip you've been on so often that you don't have to think hard to find your way, that means you've experienced this trance.

Medium Trance: Level three of trance states is about being in the zone. This is also known as the flow state. In this state, you're unaware of the passage of time, your surroundings, and even your body.

Deep Trance: This is level four, and you experience it when you're in the normal sleep state or having hypnagogia, which is the point where you're falling asleep and begin to witness shapes and colors that pop in and out of your mind's eye, among other sorts of images. You experience hypnagogia when your conscious mind begins to lose control and wind down for the day. You may also notice that your mind will concoct the weirdest stories at this point, and you may feel or hear hallucinations and even feel the sensation of falling even though you're lying on your bed.

Very Deep Trance: Level five is the last level. At this point, you no longer have conscious awareness. You're not even having dreams but are comatose for all intents and purposes.

Why Does Trance Matter?

When it comes to spirit work, the best levels of trance to work with are from levels two to four. You need to be in a trance state when working with spirits because this state of consciousness makes it possible to silence the critical conscious mind, which tends to interfere with spiritual communication. Put yourself into a trance first because your rational, conscious mind likes to act as an obstacle to the subconscious mind. Your ego is meant to keep you safe from anything it thinks is a threat which, according to your ego, is anything that would threaten its own existence. The problem with the ego is that it makes it tough for you to get rid of toxic habits, learn new, better ones, and go deeper in your spiritual practice because it worries you may experience a loss of ego or ego death. Your ego will use every tool to frustrate your spiritual work, including splitting, projection, denial, and repression.

Trance has always been used in spiritual work, helping people connect with their spirit guides, soul families, ancestors, and animal guides, among other beings of the spirit realm. Many theories explain how trance can help you deepen your connection with the spirit. Still, the most plausible one is that everyone's subconscious mind is connected, creating something called the Collective subconscious, a concept suggested by Carl Jung. It's also called the Deep Mind or Universal Mind. Through the Deep Mind, we can connect with any energy we want.

How to Enter a Trance State

You can use the following methods to get into a trance state, whether the light trance or the deep trance state. The way you work with these methods is up to you, but please note that if you struggle with schizoaffective disorder, schizophrenia, or any other sort of mental illness that is deeply troublesome, you should check with your medical professional first to be sure it's okay to practice these things.

Use breath work: When you breathe in a certain pattern and at a certain pace, you're likely to change your state of consciousness. There are several yogic breathing practices (breathwork) that you can use to help you. For instance, pranayama is breathwork meant to help you get rid of stumbling stones on an emotional and mental level in your life. It can also create a trance state. Try *udgeeth pranayama*. Udgeeth means "deep and rhythmic chanting," and pranayama means "breathwork," "breathing exercises," or "breath and energy mastery." With this particular form of pranayama, you'll chant the Om mantra in a rhythm. Om is pronounced like "home" but without the letter h. Here are the steps:

1. Sit somewhere comfortable, preferably on a stable surface. Keep an elongated spine. A folded blanket beneath your hips can be excellent support if you sit on the floor. Plant both feet on the floor firmly and flatly if you use a chair.

2. Close your eyes or keep a soft gaze.

3. Begin breathing deeply through the nose as you let your body relax. Check your face, neck, and shoulders to be sure you're not holding tension there.

4. As you breathe, ensure only your belly moves up and down on each inhale and exhale.

5. Do your best to ensure the exhales are longer than the inhales, and don't strain while you breathe.

6. While breathing, chant the Om and pay attention to how the mantra vibrates. Also, notice how your breath feels. You want to chant loud enough to hear yourself and feel the vibration but softly enough to remain focused on your breath simultaneously.

7. Keep chanting while you breathe slowly, and keep your attention on your breath. When you're ready to come out of it, take a moment to sit in silence so you can absorb all you've received from the spiritual experience.

Use Mantras: A mantra is a sound or word you repeat to get into a trance. It's not the same thing as praying, which only leads to a light trance state since you'll need your conscious mind to pray. If you're drawn to prayer, you could try different ways, such as using a language you make up as you go, a different language than you're used to, and so on. Doing it this way will help you bypass your conscious, rational mind.

Try Shamanic Drumming and Sounds: Shamans work with drums because they help to put the spiritual people into a state of trance so they can begin their shamanic journeys. You could buy a little drum (like a bongo or a hand drum) or work with some shamanic drumming sounds online. The best sounds are repetitive and have no vocals. If you pick sounds with vocals, it's best to opt for something that isn't in your language and, therefore, cannot distract you. Other excellent tools to use are binaural and isochronic beats.

Look Up: This method is simple. Sit somewhere quiet and comfortable where you won't be bothered or distracted, and then look at something above your eye level. Keep your gaze fixed on that point, and as you do so, notice the walls and other objects in your peripheral vision while simultaneously maintaining your attention on the spot just above you. Hold this gaze for no less than five minutes.

Hypnotize Yourself: Self-hypnosis is an amazing tool to get into a trance and do your spiritual work. It's more powerful than most realize, and it's safe because you're the one in charge of how deeply you go into your trance, and no one can make you do anything you don't already want to do. To hypnotize yourself, stay in a dark room. Make sure all is quiet, and there will be no distractions or disturbances. Lie down and pay attention to your breath. In your mind, say to yourself over and over, "Sleep... Sleep... Deep sleep... Deep sleep..." Do this for several minutes, as slowly as possible. In time, you'll find that your body feels lighter and warmer than usual, and your mind will go completely quiet. At this point, you're in a trance.

Use a Pendulum: You can swing the pendulum back and forth in front of you to send you into a trance state. Just sit somewhere quiet and comfortable, and then move your attention to your pendulum. You can give it a gentle swing to begin its movement, or you can use the pendulum to move (it will move because of the ideomotor effect). You should do this for five to ten minutes and find yourself in a trance.

Now You're in Trance

Ideally, before getting into the trance state, you should be clear about your intentions for communicating with spirits. Here are some ideas you may want to pursue:

- You may want to ask the spirits questions about their own lives
- You may have questions about a specific situation you're dealing with in your life
- You can ask them for clarity about what to do next
- You can ask them about universal truths, such as the laws of manifestation
- You may ask the spirits to show you what you most need to know at the moment
- You can let them know you're willing to be a channel for them to speak through on your behalf or someone else's behalf
- You can request that they flow healing energy through you and to you mentally, physically, or emotionally
- You may assign them a task to help you stop someone who's frustrating you in their tracks

Whatever your intentions or questions are, have them in your mind as you slip into a trance. When you do, the next thing is to restate that intention or ask the question aloud and then sit and wait expectantly. If you've chosen to use automatic writing, you should be ready with your pen and paper. If you're channeling the spirit's answers, you'll find it useful to have the sound recorder app on your phone open and ready to go.

Some sessions don't require you to ask any questions of the spirits. In those cases, you can simply sit with them in silent communion. If it's an intention, you'll know they've decided to help you with it when you get an inner knowing or other messages from them that what you desire is a done deal. Then you can sit in appreciation for some more time or get out of trance.

Exiting the Trance State

It's not enough to know how to get into a trance. You've got to know how to get out of it too. When you've finished working with the spirits, you should thank them and let them know their presence is no longer needed – unless they're friendly spirits like your ancestors or a loved one. If they are other spirits you're unfamiliar with, you must thank them and instruct them to leave your space. After that, return your attention to your breath and allow yourself to slowly come back to consciousness by paying attention to the sounds around you, how you feel in your body, and anything else that can connect you with the material world. Feel the ground beneath your feet, notice what your mouth tastes like, and feel what it's like to be present. Finally, if you close your eyes, you can now open them. If you had them open with a soft gaze, you could slowly allow the room around you to come into focus.

Cleansing Yourself and Your Space

At the end of the spirit communication, cleaning yourself and your space is important. This is because you don't want any lingering, residual energy that could act as a magnet, attracting the spirits back to your space where they may decide to take agency and do whatever they want, which may not always be the best thing for you. So, you can't skip the process of cleansing yourself and your home or the space you communicated with the spirit. Here's how:

Use Salt Water: When you've finished with the spirit channeling and know they've gone, you may spritz yourself with salt water from a spritzer bottle. Salt can purify energy and eliminate any stale or bad energy around you. You should also spritz this water around your home. If you don't have a spritz bottle, simply make sure you have a bowl of water with some salt in it before you begin the session. Then when you've finished, you can dip your hand in the bowl of salt water and then flick your fingers over yourself to get the water on your body. Then, flick the water into the air around your space to cleanse the area. If you like, you can also take a bath with salt water and wash the clothes you used to reach out to the spirits with salt water, too.

Use an Egg: Egg cleansing is a practice that is well-known by many cultures across the world. All you have to do is take an uncooked egg and then begin to rub it against your body, starting from the crown of your head, and work your way down to your feet. Ensure you use downward strokes. It should be like pushing the energy away from your body and down to the ground. Make sure you don't bring the egg back up to any part of your body that you've already touched. When you've finished doing this, you can use the same egg to cleanse the room by walking from corner to corner with it held up in the air until you've covered the entire perimeter of your living space. Then, take the egg outside your home, and break it.

The Green Candle Method: Some people use a green candle for its cleansing properties. Just light it and walk around your space, again taking it to each corner until you've covered the whole perimeter of your living space. Then, like you used the egg cleansing method, break the green candle, which will release its energy into the atmosphere to clear your space.

A Final Note

When reaching out to the spirits through trance, you need to know that you may not have success on the first try or even the first few tries. It's important to be patient with yourself. Just continue to practice, and sooner or later, you'll begin receiving messages from the other side. Also, it has to be stated once more that you must avoid any negative entity. Don't seek them out. If someone comes to you for help reaching out to a spirit that was a bad person in their past life, the odds are you'll get an intuitive nudge not to do it. Honor that nudge every time it pops up. Also, if it turns out you're connecting with a spirit, and something feels off, close the connection immediately by telling them politely but firmly that they are to leave your space as you're closing the session right away. Don't wait for a response because you don't need their permission to end the session. End it, cleanse yourself and your space, and ask for the protection of your friendly ancestor spirits

Spirit communication can be an exciting and empowering experience. Still, it's important to ensure that you have the proper tools and knowledge to do it. If you don't have the right safety precautions, that excitement could quickly turn into anxiety or fear.

A trance state is a psychological state considered a heightened level of cognitive functioning in hypnosis where people appear more suggestible than usual. Several advantages come from entering this state before communicating with spirits. One of them is detaching the conscious mind from all external stimuli and thoughts, making for a much more pleasant overall experience. Other advantages include the following:

- **Lowering your fear and anxiety**, making it easier to stay in the moment and connect with spirits. The subconscious mind is what will be talking to spirits, so you don't want your conscious mind to interfere with or overthink it. You want your subconscious mind to be as clear and focused as possible so you can get past your initial fears of spirit communication and find the comfort level you need to get answers from those who have passed on.

- **Clearing out all doubt** in your mind about spirit communication. If you have a negative thought about spirits and spirit communication beforehand, feelings of fear, anxiety, and doubt will affect you. These thoughts are too strong to overcome by your conscious mind alone. So having that subconscious mind cleared out before hitting the ground running will make things much easier for you. This is why you should get into a trance.

Chapter 5: Spiritual Tools and How to Use Them

Some practitioners believe you shouldn't use tools to communicate with spirits, but that's not the case. If you're a beginner, you'll find the tools especially useful for your practice, as they'll make it much easier to open up a line of communication with the spirit world. There are several tools you could work with. Check each one out to find what resonates with you the best, and use only that one unless your intuition tells you it's time to try something else. Here are some of the tools:

Not only can you use the pendulum to help you diagnose energetic and spiritual problems, but you can also use it to make decisions and connect with spirits.

- The pendulum
- The Ouija board
- Paper and pen (for channeled or automatic writing)
- Mirror (for scrying)
- A bowl of water (for scrying)
- Candles and incense sticks (also for scrying)

No matter which tool you're working with, ensure you cleanse it with salt water or smudge it with sage. You should also charge the tools. You can do this by letting the tools sit out in the sunlight, under the full moon, or simply by placing your hands over them and envisioning or feeling good energy flowing from your hands into the tools. Now it's time to look at how to use each one.

Communicating with the Pendulum

The pendulum can be of any material. Some are just necklaces with a charm, crystal, or weighty items you can swing. The item mustn't be too heavy or too light. Preferably, it should be half an ounce. The best pendulums have a weight that tapers off into a point and is about six inches. If you don't want to buy one, you can make it yourself with any makeshift string and objects like keys as the weight. Not only can you use the pendulum to help you diagnose energetic and spiritual problems, but you can also use it to make decisions and connect with spirits. You can even use it to find things you've lost. Here's how to use a pendulum correctly.

Figure Out Its Programming

First, you want to know how your pendulum swings when it tells you yes, no, or maybe. You should ensure that no one is around to disturb or bother you while you work this out. Also, ensure that you're in the right frame of mind (not upset or tired), so you don't misinterpret your answers. Since your intention is to use the pendulum to interact with the spirit, it is best to treat your pendulum right and handle the process with reverence.

Sit at a table or a desk, and lean on it with your elbow to support it. The elbow should belong to your dominant hand. Hold the pendulum in that hand between your thumb and index finger, and let it swing on its own. Then you can ask the pendulum, "Show me yes," and wait to see which way it swings. If it doesn't swing, you've got no reply. Move on to the next request, "Show me no." This is because some pendulums prefer to answer one question first instead of the other. The pendulum may move back and forth, left and right, in big or little circles. Note its answers as you ask it. You should also ask it to show you "I don't know" and "Maybe." If you prefer, you can draw a circle on a piece of paper, split it into four quadrants, and label each quadrant "Yes," "No," "Maybe," and "I don't know."

When you've worked out the directions, ask some simple questions you already know the answers to as a warm-up to be sure that everything's working as it should.

Get Into a State of Trance

This is to put you in the vibration where you can summon the energy of the spirits you want to interact with and keep your mind focused on your intentions and questions.

Ask the Spirit If They're Present

Your pendulum should swing to let you know. You can also use your pendulum chart to find out by letting the pendulum hang over each word. Wherever it begins to move, that's your answer.

Ask the Spirit Whatever You Want to Know

Obviously, you're limited to yes and no questions unless you want to create a pendulum chart with every letter of the alphabet (in which case, perhaps an Ouija board would be more appropriate).

When you've finished, thank the spirits and close the session, then cleanse yourself, your pendulum, and your space.

Communicating through the Ouija Board

The Ouija board is an easy way to connect with spirits. Many are nervous about this board, as they think it's a portal through which malevolent forces can come. There's reason to be careful with this board, though. If you'd never leave your home door unlocked every time you went out, then you should be mindful of not ending a session properly. When you want to connect to the spirit world through the Ouija board (or any other tool), you've got to know exactly with whom you want to communicate. If you didn't like a certain person when they were alive, the odds are you're not going to want to hear from them just because they've passed on. So be clear

about your intentions first. You can buy a board or make one
yourself.

How to Make Your Ouija Board

1. Get a large piece of paper and write "Yes" at the top left and
   "No" at the top right.
2. Beneath the words "Yes" and "No," write out each letter of the
   alphabet in a slight arc. Let the first set of letters be from A to M
   and the second set be from N to Z.
3. At the bottom left-hand side of the paper, write "Hello," and at
   the bottom right, write "Goodbye."
4. Draw a circle above the word "Yes" and put dashes around it,
   so you've got a sun with rays.
5. Draw a crescent moon above the word "No" and draw rays
   emanating from it.
6. For the planchette, work with an upside-down glass.

Using the Ouija Board

Set the mood: The room you're using should be dark. Candlelight is a
good idea, as spirits will be drawn to the flames and fire energy.
Eliminate all distractions and put away all phones and other devices.

Set the board up: You can let it rest on your knees.

Do a warm-up: To warm up the board, move the planchette to
form the infinity or figure of eight symbol.

**Figure out who you want to connect with, then enter into a state of
trance:** When you know the spirit you want to reach out to, you can
use whichever method is best for you to get into a trance state.

**Ask them if they're present, and when they confirm, ask them your
questions:** When asking them questions, do your best to be polite to
your guests. Note that you can get rid of them if they're rude to you,
taunt you, or ruin the séance you're holding.

Write down all the messages they give you: In time, you may notice
that you're starting to fill in the blanks for them because you're
channeling the information in real-time and much faster than you can
move the planchette. Write it all down because it will definitely prove
useful information. Note that sometimes the spirits make spelling

errors. That's perfectly fine.

When you're done, thank them for their time, and send them on the way: You can thank them for taking the time and effort it took them to connect with you. Then tell them to be on their way and leave your space.

Cleanse yourself and your space: Use any of the methods mentioned earlier.

Extra Tips: Don't use the Ouija board alone if you are over-excited. The odds are that if you're very excited, you may want to ask too many questions. In a group, you may confuse the spirit if everyone asks questions at once. Let this be a turn-by-turn situation.

Another tip is never to ask questions to discover things you shouldn't, like when or how you'll die. Most spirits will not give you a serious answer. Don't waste your time asking questions you've already figured out the answers to. And you want to ensure that the spirit guest with you isn't trying to take over the session because you summoned it for answers, not to be lectured into oblivion.

Just because something came through the board doesn't mean it's true, so you must check in with your gut and practice discernment to be safe. Only take what truly resonates from the message and eliminate the rest. There will be times when the séance doesn't work out. And that's fine. Spirits are like humans in that sometimes they don't feel chatty. Don't take it personally. Just try another time again.

Communicating through Automatic Writing

1. First, know what you want to get out of this interaction.
2. Clear your mind and ground yourself.
3. Get a paper and pen sheet, or open up a new document on your computer.
4. Get into a trance state.
5. Say "Hello" to the spirit, and then ask it your questions.
6. Allow your hand to write as it will. Don't judge anything you get.
7. When you've finished asking, thank the spirits and then ask them to leave.
8. Cleanse yourself and your ritual space.

9. Now, analyze what you've written in the book. If you don't think you wrote anything serious, don't worry about it. With time, you'll get clearer, better information using this method. Just make sure to practice often.

Some of the messages that come through may make sense in terms of sentence structure, but their meaning may not be clear right away or until later when something happens; then, you may suddenly know what it was about. After the session, you may ponder these automatic writings, but don't beat yourself up for not knowing. Trust that all will be revealed.

Communication through Scrying

Scrying involves looking at a reflective object to see things in it. You may see images, words, the past, the present, the future, and more. Scrying is a craft practiced with various mediums like lakes, bowls of water, fire, brass, copper, smoke, etc. Nowadays, many diviners who scry use scrying mirrors, also known as black mirrors. If you'd like to make yours, you can get the materials you need from a thrift store. Most of the mirrors are round, but you can go for something square if you like. You'll need a picture frame with a piece of glass. The glass will serve as your reflective surface.

1. Clean the glass with a window cleaner, freeing it from smudges and stains.

2. Put the glass on the newspaper. You only need a sheet.

3. Paint the glass black with some acrylic paint. It's best to go for the paint that will leave you with a metallic or glossy finish, but if you only have matte paint, that's fine too. You may need to do a few thin coats, waiting for each one to dry before applying the next coat. Make sure there's no spot uncovered, and you don't leave streaks. Five coats should do it, so you can no longer see through the paint if you hold the glass up against the light.

4. Put the glass back in the frame with the painted side as the back. The clear glass should be to the front.

5. Clean the glass once more to remove all streaks, and you've finished.

You can buy it online if you don't want to make yours.

How to Scry with Your Scrying Mirror

1. Cleanse your mirror by smudging it with some sage. This will eliminate any energies that are old, stale, and bad.

2. Bless your mirror and charge it by letting your hands hover over it and imagining a ball of white light moving from your hands to your mirror. Imagine feeling good energy flowing from your hands to the mirror if you can't visualize. You can also charge it in sunlight or under the moonlight during a full moon.

3. When you're ready to use your mirror, ensure there is not much light in the room. You can draw the shades and then light candles on either side of the mirror. Alternatively, you can just dim the lights.

4. Set your mirror up, so it's at an angle that keeps you from reflecting on it.

5. Ground yourself, and then take some minutes to get into a trance.

6. When your mind is clear and empty, gaze into the mirror. If you've got a question to ask, you may do so. Note that you want to look through the mirror or past it instead of right at it. At first, you may see nothing, but you'll notice colors with time. The images you get may not be clear initially, but with time and practice, you'll find they become clearer.

7. Practice for ten to fifteen minutes each time in the beginning, then you can try for longer later. Note that sometimes you may not get an image, but you'll get an intuitive nudge about what you're looking for.

8. Keep a pen and paper close to your mirror to note the important things you see as soon as you've finished scrying.

Chapter 6: Working with Ancestors and Departed Loved Ones

Now that you know all the necessary information about communicating with spirits, it's time to learn how to contact certain kinds of spirits. In this chapter, you'll learn how to connect with your ancestors and the loved ones you had who have passed on.

Many people come across ancestral spirits without realizing it.
https://www.pexels.com/photo/man-hands-people-woman-7189444/

Have you ever felt a chill in the air or sensed someone standing behind you? Have you ever looked over your shoulder and thought someone was there, only to find that nobody was there? You're not crazy. Our ancestors' spirits live with us every day.

Many people come across ancestral spirits without realizing it. It's probably best to have an open mind about these encounters because they can be powerful and positive. When you communicate with your spiritual ancestors, it feels like they are right next to you, asking you to let them be a helpful, positive part of your life. No matter how old or young you are — and whether you believe in supernatural forces or not — it's healthy to interact with the spirits of your family members who have passed from this world.

Ancestral spirits are more than imaginary friends and guardians. They're a living part of your history, part of your heritage. According to Native American traditions, they are a bridge between the dead and the living, and they talk to us so that we can share our stories with them.

Benefits of Connecting with Ancestors

Ancestral spirits can help you to heal from past hurts. Talking with your spirit guides or ancestral spirits is a great way to heal past wounds. These spirits are the guardians of your family lineage, which takes you back to the beginning of your tribe. Talking with them allows you to connect with everything that your ancestors went through and how much they suffered and struggled from living in a different era. Your ancestors' spirits are deeply connected to their stories and want us to talk about them so we can learn from their struggles and mistakes.

Ancestral spirits can free you from negative thoughts or emotions like fear, anger, or other painful feelings. It's not uncommon for people to feel emotions they don't want or need to. An ancestral spirit can help you to let go of negative thoughts and feelings that might be holding you back from other goals in your life.

An ancestral spirit can support you in reaching your goals, whether it's a career, spiritual growth, or anything else important to you. An ancestral spirit can help bring your dreams into reality. This happens when our ancestors are given a voice, and the spirits speak directly and powerfully into our lives, giving us strength and the inner resolve we need to make our dreams come true.

Ancestral spirits can tell you exactly what you need to hear. When we ask our ancestors' spirits to talk with us, they don't give us platitudes or say, "Everything's going to be okay." Rather, they are brutally honest and will not hold back any truth. Sometimes this can be painful, but often the words we need to hear most are the ones that hurt us the most.

Connecting with Your Ancestors

Before you get into the process of reaching out to your ancestors, the first thing you should consider doing is looking into your genealogical tree. If this isn't possible for you, don't sweat it. It's just an optional step that can be useful for establishing a connection with your ancestors. For instance, learning about who they are might help you know their favorite things, so you know what offerings to make to them that would please them. Here are some tips for finding out about your roots:

Organize What You Learn

Your first weeks will give you many results, and you'll need a way to organize what you learn. You should use an online genealogical database to help you before you start your research. You can find many for free or at a fee, including the popular Ancestry.com, an excellent choice because tens of millions of family trees are on their database. The branches may be useful to you as you search.

Look for Clues in Your Home

You should consider everything around you. Look out for patterns and check out your family history. Some clues about who you are could be hidden in plain sight. You can check out the basement, drawers, the attic, personal documents, letters, and anything else that's in storage that may help. Look at dated items and documents, and check your family albums and memorabilia. Look at diaries, report cards, and so on. You should get your relatives involved in the process and let them know your motivation.

Speak with the Elders

Older relatives will have more information than you do. The older, the better, as they'll act as a link to previous generations you may not have met. Even when you've got the facts about your entire family, you should ask your elders questions and record them because they may give you even more important details. Seek their help to identify faces and places in old pictures, as this could lead to stories that give you even more information to work with. Ask about your grandparents, great-grandparents, and other relatives. Ask for full names, siblings, where they were born, when they were born, their ethnicities and nationalities, what they did for a living, where they were buried, and so on. Be respectful as you ask these questions. If someone refuses to answer certain things, you should move on to something else rather than persist and offend them. You may be able to find the missing pieces through your own research.

Use the Internet

Now that you've got all the information from questioning your relatives and sleuthing at home, it's time to turn to the Internet. You can use different services, resources, and more to help you with your genealogy. FamilySearch is a good free resource, run by the Mormon Church, and is a nonprofit. They've been in the business of collecting records globally for the past 100 years, and they update their online records with tens of millions of entries each week. Look into their books, publications, microfilm catalog, etc.

Get a DNA Test

National Geographic offers Geno 2.0, a kit that can help you discover more about who you are without needing to follow a paper trail. You'll learn about how your ancient ancestors migrated eons ago and where your roots truly are. You want a DNA testing service with an impressive database of already tested people and the option to store your DNA samples for free in case you'd like another test later. You should beware of your decision to get tested, as you may learn a lot about your immediate family members or yourself that you're not prepared for.

Socialize

Social media will be good for you in this case. You can connect with people with the same surnames as you and also look for local organizations, archives, and genealogical services present in your ancestor's original hometown. You'll find it very useful to speak to strangers you share the last name with if they haven't had to deal with too many people asking those same questions.

Keep a Handle on Your Expectations

Most TV shows tend to sensationalize the process of discovering genealogy information. As a result, some people think they'll find out they were related to some great person who lived in the past. The odds are your origins are very ordinary, and there's nothing wrong with that. Those people still made a difference in the world because, after all, is said and done, you wouldn't be here without them.

Don't Quit

Finding out about your roots is very rewarding. When you put in the time and work and continue to push through despite obstacles, you'll be glad you did. This is because you'll be able to establish a richer connection with your ancestors. If you're wondering how long the process will take, remember that the more you look into your past, the more ancestors you'll learn about. In other words, the process of discovering your lineage never ends. So enjoy it. When you begin connecting with your ancestral spirits, you can ask them questions you've been unable to find the answers to. They'll be more than happy to fill in the blanks since you've taken such a deep interest in them and their lives.

How to Connect with Your Ancestor Spirits

Here's a ritual you can use to connect with your ancestor spirits.

1. **Begin by grounding yourself**: You must have the right energy to perform this ritual. Therefore, it is important to ground yourself. Are you feeling tired or not quite present? You should use the grounding ritual from the previous chapter to draw energy from the earth to fuel you. Feeling all over the place and overly excited? Or do you feel like you have picked up other people's energies over the day? Then let the earth absorb the energy from you as you ground yourself.

2. **Cleanse the space you'll be working with:** Burn sage and smudge the room, walking from one corner to the next. Alternatively, you could sprinkle or spritz salt water all over the space or create a circle with salt on the floor around the area you'll be working in. This is meant to keep out any negative or unwanted energies around you.

3. **Cleanse the tools you intend to work with:** All you have to do is use sage or saltwater. Make sure you have your pen and paper or other tools ready to take notes as soon as you're done channeling your ancestral spirits or connecting with them. After cleansing them, set them up for use.

4. **Cleanse yourself:** When you've cleansed the space, cleanse yourself by smudging with sage or using salt water. If you like, you can draw a protective symbol on your forehead with your forefinger after dipping it into salt water or the ashes left behind by the burnt sage.

5. **Get into a trance:** Begin by focusing on your breath in meditation, and then follow your instructions earlier in the book. Keep your intention in the back of your mind as you slip into a trance.

6. **Feel for the energy of your ancestors:** Now you're in a trance. Seek out your ancestors by connecting with their energy. By sitting in silence, you can tell when they're around. There may be a charge in the air, a change in pressure, some sound, or other things.

7. **Set their offerings before them:** If you know what your ancestors enjoy, you can offer it to them. You'll know what to give them if you do your homework on who they were and what they were like when they were alive. The offerings should already be there with you, so just declare that you've brought them gifts to honor them and thank them for showing up.

8. **Ask your questions:** When you sense they're present, you may go ahead to work with them using your tools, whether that's the Ouija board, your pen and paper (for automatic writing), your sound recorder (for channeling), your black mirror for scrying, and so on. Ask them your questions and expect them to give you answers. Don't push, and don't be impatient. It will take them as long as it takes them.

9. **Express gratitude and make your requests:** Thank them for the answers that they've given you. Use the opportunity to ask them for anything else you'd like from them, whether that's health, provision, protection, guidance, abundance, or anything else. Then, thank them once more for being there for you.

10. Let them know you're done: Since these are your ancestors, you don't have to dismiss them. However, if you want to, you can simply tell them at the end of the session that they should leave now. They'll respect your boundaries and do just that. This is the close of the session. If you don't ask them to leave, don't be surprised at phenomena happening around you as they love to let you know that they're always with you.

You can use these same steps to connect with other loved ones you know who have passed on. In the beginning, these conversations with spirit may feel one-sided, but you must keep going. Continue reaching out to them each day, and with time, you'll begin to actually receive information from them, making your effort worth it.

Why Gratitude Matters

In real life, you probably don't care much for friends who only show up when they need something from you, only to disappear once more without as much as a *thank you.* If you have a healthy self-esteem, you realize those aren't friends – they are leeches.

This is why you must express gratitude to the spirits who come to your aid. It's also why offerings are so important. If you don't know what the spirits want because you didn't get that information from your research or there was too little information to go on, just let your gut guide you about what to offer. You may offer food, drink, water, cigarettes, money, fruit, flowers, or anything else your intuition leads you to. If your intentions are pure and you've made an offering, trust that the spirits see your heart and appreciate you for trying. They may even offer information about what would make a suitable offering for subsequent channeling sessions.

Helpful Tips to Keep Your Ancestors and Deceased Loved Ones Around

1. **Say hello to them** first thing in the morning. Say out loud, "Good morning, my ancestors. Thank you for keeping me safe during the night." Let them know how you'd like them to help you throughout the day.

2. **Establish a special place in your home** where you can go to talk with your ancestral spirits. It could be a small room, a

kitchen corner, or even a special chair dedicated only to these conversations.

3. **Leave an empty seat at the dinner table** for deceased loved ones. Maybe it's someone who died before you were born or a relative who has recently passed away. Use your imagination to see them sitting across from you at the breakfast table. Speak with them and make them feel welcome.

4. **Pray**. Praying is a wonderful way to open yourself up and speak with your ancestors' spirits. It creates a spiritual field in which they can come closer to you and connect with you even more.

5. **Call on them during times of need**. Call on the ancestors for guidance and advice whenever you're feeling confused or unsure of what decisions are right for you. They will help you find the answers you need and show you the path ahead that's best for your journey in life.

6. **Set up altars in your home**. Altars help you to remember your family lineage and show respect for beloved ancestors who have already passed on. An ancestral altar can be as simple or elaborate as you'd like it to be. It's an attractive place where you can leave offerings for them and keep pictures of those who have preceded you in this world.

7. **Visit their gravesites**. Make sure you take them flowers and fresh water whenever there is cause to celebrate their memory - a birthday, anniversary, a religious holiday, or the first day of summer or winter, for example. They'll appreciate that special touch of recognition from their descendants today just as much as they did when they were alive and well on the Earth plane.

8. **Make a homemade memorial plaque**. You can create one you hang on your wall or one in the front window of your home to honor your ancestors. Convey thoughts of gratitude and love for them every time you see it. Then, whenever someone passes through your home, they'll see it and think of the special relationship between you and the spirits who have already passed over.

9. **Create a space for them** in the house where all their important belongings will always be displayed, so their spirit is never far from where they were born and lived. Place their personal items on a shelf with a photo of them, create small altars, or all of the above. They'll love to see this spot every time they visit you. Take fresh flowers from your garden and fresh water whenever you can.

10. **Honor their memory at Thanksgiving**, Christmas, birthdays, and other holidays are times when many ancestral spirits like to come back and visit the ones who remain. This is a good time to ask that they give you signs that they are still around by moving something around in your home, hearing the rustling of leaves where there are no trees nearby, or seeing animals behaving strangely when you're thinking about them.

Chapter 7: Connect to Your Spirit Guides

Who are spirit guides? These divine beings are either assigned to people or chosen to help them grow spiritually, keep them safe, and guide them along their journey. Some believe that spirit guides aren't actual beings but are more psychological projections representing parts of the human subconscious, helping us feel whole. However, spirit guides are much more than that. They are real. You may think of them as being aspects of your Higher Self, if you like, coming to you at different times in your life to offer love, support, insight, protection, and much more.

You may think of spirit guides as being aspects of your Higher Self.

You may have just one guide or several. Your guide may be someone who once lived on Earth or hasn't at all. You may also have animal spirit guides. Regardless of what you make of the concept of spirit guides, the fact remains that everyone needs some support and direction in life. You would be hard-pressed to find a better being to provide this than your spirit guide. Your guide can offer you help that no one else possibly could, making it a worthwhile endeavor to connect to them. Spirit guides tend to make their presence known when you're about to experience a significant change in your life or when you need to be quickly rescued from something. You will also notice them when you're experiencing a rebirth and new things you may be afraid of.

Spirit guides are part of the forces of the universe that are meant to lend us their help. Your guide may be an entity from a different world, a god or goddess, a mythical creature, an animal, an angel, and so on. Living a life without being conscious of your guide is incredibly empty, and you'll begin to wonder why you didn't reach out sooner by the time you've read this chapter. Your spirit guide will show you what you need to know about yourself, others, and the world. They'll comfort you as no one else can, support you through thick and thin, lead you away from danger, warn you when something's off, teach you things you need to know to progress in life, and so on.

How Many Guides Do You Have?

You may wonder how many guides you have. Do you only get one? Often, it's the case that we all have more than one guide or at least more than one aspect of that energy. Some of the guides you have were assigned to you at birth. However, others come into your life later. It depends on what you're going through and what phase of your life you are facing. You may think of your guides as being split into two groups:

1. Major guides.
2. Minor guides.

The major guides you have will help you with your life path. They're there to help you with the main life lessons you're supposed to learn and your ultimate purpose for incarnating on Earth. On the other hand, the minor guides only stick around briefly to help with fleeting, daily issues that may give you trouble.

The Role of Your Guide in Your Spiritual Awakening

Your spirit guides have a major role in helping you awaken to higher and higher levels of spiritual awareness. Your spirit guide is meant to help you with your spiritual evolution. For instance, assume one of your guides is the Bodhisattva of compassion named Kuan Yin. The odds are he will show you how to be more compassionate and merciful to others and yourself. If you're drawn to the Norse goddess Frejya, she may be asking you to learn to make peace with your sexuality and to accept the facts of life and death. With Ganesha, the Indian deity with the elephant head, you'll learn how to be wise, clear in thoughts, generous, and prudent with abundance. Your guides can help you improve, especially regarding the emotional wounds, traumas, and cognitive dissonance you suffer in different life aspects. They can help you eliminate blocks in your energy that keep you small and feeling lifeless.

How to Connect with Your Spirit Guides

Dreamwork

1. The first thing to do with dreamwork is to work on your dream recall. To do this, every night before you go to bed, suggest you'll remember all your dreams in detail. Make sure you have a dream journal, a pen by your bed, or a dream journaling app on your phone.

2. When you wake up from a dream, don't move a muscle. Just sit and think about the last thing, scene, or feeling you remember from the dream. Then work your way backward until you remember everything. It is important not to move because if you do, you'll ruin the process of recalling your dreams.

3. Immediately after you've finished with dream recall, you have to write down your dream in your journal or record it. Start by writing or saying a few keywords that remind you of each aspect of your dreams, so you don't forget as you're writing. Then you can flesh out the details of each keyword after you've got them all down on paper.

4. When your dream recall improves significantly, it's time for a new suggestion. Suggest to yourself every night before bed that you'll connect with your spirit guides. It may happen the first night or several later. However, it's going to happen. You can note things you want to ask them and write the answers in your journal as soon as you awaken.

5. Note their energy signatures. This way, you can seek them out in your waking life by feeling for that energy and holding it.

Affirmations

Affirmations are positive statements that you repeat to yourself frequently. Repeating them over and over again can help change the thoughts you think of yourself, which in turn will help you change your behavior. When you communicate with your guides, affirm that it is a positive and good experience. Use affirmations when you wake up in the morning or evening before going to sleep. You can also write them down for later use and read them whenever it is convenient. Affirmations are meant to help change your subconscious assumptions so that you achieve a state of greater self-esteem, happiness, health, and well-being. You can affirm that you always easily connect with your spirit guides and receive their messages clearly and often before using affirmations. Putting yourself in a light trance before starting is best.

Bibliomancy

Bibliomancy, or divination through books, has been around since ancient times. You'll be able to receive guidance as long as you have a choice of books on hand. You can choose a book about the skills and knowledge you want to acquire. It's also important that you keep it near you at all times. Bibliomancy is an effective way in which to communicate with your guides effectively and safely. Bibliomancy involves asking your guides for guidance and getting the answer to your questions through the words in the book. You can use it, especially when you're new to spirit work or having difficulty gathering enough information about something. You can read different books, think of specific questions you have, and ask them with faith that the answers that come back will help you in some way. Here's how to use this method:

1. Ground yourself.

2. Cleanse yourself, your space, and your book.

3. Sit and get into a trance state.

4. Focus on your intention to connect with your spirit guides.

5. When you feel their presence, bring your question to mind and ask it.

6. Hold the book out in front of you and sit with your eyes closed while you continue to focus on the question.

7. When you feel the spirits are ready for you, open the book to any random page. Read the first thing your eyes fall on, whether at the top, bottom, or middle of the page.

Candle Work

Candles are powerful. They involve the element of fire, and you can use the power of fire to connect you to the subtle energies of your spirit guides. Here is an explanation:

1. **Obtain candles**: If you don't have a burning need for candles, you can easily find them at your local supermarket or craft store. The easiest way to obtain candles is to buy various colors, sizes, and shapes. You can also opt to use tea lights.

2. **Create a safe space**: It's also crucial that while you're performing candle work, you create a safe space where no one can disturb you. You must turn off the phones so no one will disturb or distract your train of thought. You should also position yourself somewhere comfortable where you won't be distracted or bothered by outside forces.

3. **Ground yourself:** Grounding yourself before connecting with your spirit guides is also a good idea. Grounding is like a preparation for connecting with your guides. It's an age-old practice meant to ensure that you won't be pulled into the astral plane while being susceptible to energies that shouldn't be there. Grounding can help you prepare for your connection with your spirit guides and protect you from any unwanted or malicious entities. The simplest way to ground yourself is by taking deep breaths, visualizing white light surrounding your body, and encasing it in white light.

4. **Light the candles:** Once you've created a safe space, it's time to light them using a lighter or matches. The number of candles you light should be based on your intuition. Place the candles around in a circle. You must treat the candles with respect, especially because they have a symbolic meaning and represent your spiritual connection to certain forces in the universe.

5. **Ask for guidance:** Ask your guides to manifest before you by calling out their names as clearly and distinctly as possible. Take note of any sensations you feel to discern whether they're communicating with you. If they're already communicating with you, pay close attention to their messages, and record them in your journal later on so that you don't forget anything important.

6. **Thank your guides**: When you've finished connecting with them, thank them for what they've done and continue to do for you.

7. **Close the session:** Let your guides know that you've finished with them for the time being, and then put out the candle flames using a snuffer or let them burn down completely. Whatever you do, don't blow out the candle with your breath.

Keeping the Connection Alive

1. **Show respect**: Some people have problems with their spirit guides because they don't show them enough respect. You should never think you can talk to your guides in any way you choose. Remember that everyone has their own boundaries and limits, and this includes your guides.

2. **Ask your guides for help**: If you want to ensure that you can keep your spirit guides with you, then you should never be too shy to ask for their help or assistance whenever you need it. You can also ask for their help to maintain your friendship with them.

3. **Take time to connect with them:** Make sure you take the time to connect with them as often as you can, and you should also make sure that you always show them respect and care.

4. Maintain a spiritual journal: It's also a good idea to maintain a journal so you can record the messages from your guides and anything else that comes up in future sessions.

5. Practice gratitude: Practicing gratitude is another way to ensure that you can maintain a good connection and continue experiencing their guidance. Another important thing here is that you shouldn't be too embarrassed to express your gratitude, and this is because your guides are also grateful for the fact that you're meeting them at all.

Your spirit guides are not just characters that only come to your aid when you're in a state of distress. They're with you as allies throughout your life and should be treated with the utmost respect. You can do this by following some of the tips listed above, and by doing so, you'll be able to keep your connection with them alive.

Chapter 8: Contacting Angels

There are multitudes of angels, far too many to keep track of. The easiest of them all to reach out to is your guardian angel. But, before getting into who the guardian angel is, you need to learn who angels are in general.

There are multitudes of angels, far too many to keep track of.
https://www.pexels.com/photo/white-ceramic-figurine-of-angel-illustration-52718/

Who Is an Angel?

Angels are beings with extraordinary power who are in service of the Source that creates all worlds. They can help people in different ways. "Angel" is a word that comes from *angelos*, a Greek word that means "messenger." They act as messengers of the divine, healers, protectors, and more. When they appear on Earth, they either take on human form or show themselves in full glory. This implies that angels could be around you, showing up in disguise. They also tend to have a glow about them.

According to Islam, Christianity, and Judaism, angels are particular about serving the God responsible for creating them. In Islam, it's said that the angels are faithful in their service, but in Christianity, there are records of angels opting to rebel against their God. In Buddhism and Hinduism, and some of the forms of New Age spirituality, it's said that angels are beings who have worked their way up the totem pole of spirituality, making their way to the highest of realms by going through tests. They continue to evolve, gaining strength and wisdom even after they've achieved their status as angels.

Angels can also deliver messages from the spirit realm to those on Earth. Usually, their messages are meant to offer comfort and encouragement. At other times, they offer dire warnings to their charges to ensure they don't find themselves in dangerous situations. These divine beings also offer their protection, guarding the ones they watch over so that they don't get into any sort of danger that would prove fatal or impossible. For the longest time, many stories have been of people being rescued by angels. For instance, there have been stories of people spiraling away from an accident scene to be dropped off a short distance away and safe from harm. According to Catholicism and other religious traditions with similar views, everyone gets a guardian angel assigned to them to be there throughout their life.

Another fascinating thing that angels do is keep records of everyone's actions. According to Christian, Jewish, and some New Age beliefs, it's said that Metatron is the archangel responsible for this task, working along with the angels known as the powers. In Islam, you have the Kiraman Katibin who handles this job, and it's said that everyone has two of these, one to record the good you do, the other to record the bad. According to Sikhism, Gupta and Chitr are responsible for noting down every decision people make. Gupta writes down the decisions that no one but God knows, while Chitr writes down the actions and decisions that everyone else can see.

Who Is Your Guardian Angel?

You definitely have a guardian angel, whether you are conscious of them or not. Not believing they exist doesn't invalidate their existence. Those who don't believe in guardian angels just chalk up the times they've been saved from danger to pure luck, but the odds are their angel was there looking out for them. Some people think each person has just one guardian angel that helps them all through their life, while others believe that you get assistance from various guardian angels only as needed, which means the angel you get is the perfect one for your needs.

Your guardian angel is the best angel to reach out to when you need anything, whether it's help, advice, companionship, protection, or anything else. The reason is that they're literally assigned to help you, which means you are energetically and spiritually closer to them than any other angel. Does this mean you can't connect with other angels? Of course not. When you want to reach out to others, it's simply a matter of intention. However, even in that scenario, your guardian angel is the best one to ask for help in that regard because they will know exactly how to connect you with the other entities you may wish to commune with. Also, since they've been with you all your life, the odds are you'll be able to recognize them with ease when they're acting on your behalf. It will be much easier for you to detect their presence and, therefore, to hear their messages.

Benefits of Connecting with Your Guardian Angel

1. **Reaching out to them permits them to act on your behalf:** The thing about angels is that they may be present, but they often don't step in to do things for you because they will never violate your free will. The times they do interfere, it's often because your life is at stake, and they have to do something to save you from yourself, someone else, or a dire situation you're in. So, when you connect with them, you can give them permission to do more for you than they already do, which will improve your life.

2. **Establishing a connection makes it easier for them to give you messages that can help you in your situation:** When you connect with your guardian angel, it's as though you're opening a little window of communication between the two of you, allowing them to communicate with you in ways that are much more direct and easier to understand. They'll be able to make their presence known straightforwardly. You'll never have to second-guess yourself about which messages are just recurring thoughts or dreams and which ones are from your angel.

3. **Having a direct line of communication makes their presence much stronger:** When you connect with your guardian angel, you're giving them permission to be close to your side at all times, helping you and protecting you from harm. This will strengthen their divine presence. You'll feel safer, more secure, and much happier knowing that you're being looked out for by someone who loves and cares for you deeply. At the same time, it also increases your awareness that an angel is always watching over us.

4. **Having a guardian angel makes you feel less alone in this world:** When you know someone on your side whose sole purpose is to help and protect you, it makes you feel far less alone in the universe. It gives you a tool that helps you get through each day with ease and joy. Even if there are times when things seem bleak and bleaker still, just the knowledge that there is an angel on your side, who loves and cares for you deeply and wants only the best for your life, it helps bolster your optimism and make the most difficult of situations seem manageable.

5. **Connecting with your guardian angel increases your personal power:** A greater sense of security comes about with a greater sense of purpose. When you have a guardian angel, you have someone to turn to who can help you achieve everything your soul desires. They can give you guidance and help you along your path. Most importantly, when looking at things from this perspective, it's as if they are practically carrying half of the burden for you. All of these make it easier for them to carry out their life purpose. Those who believe in guardian angels believe that this is exactly what guardian angels are designed to do. They make our lives easier and better by taking away some of our

hardships, showing us we can handle more than we think on our own, and helping us to overcome our problems one step at a time. Knowing you're connected to your guardian angel makes you feel more secure and confident in yourself and your abilities. With their guidance, you'll be able to make better decisions, take more effective actions, and move forward with greater ease and determination. You'll also stop being fearful, automatically protecting you from negative energies, making it even easier for your angel to ward off bad luck or negativity that may affect your life.

How to Contact Your Guardian Angel

1. **Have a quiet moment alone and ground yourself:** The first step is to find a quiet place where you can be alone with your thoughts. This can be in your bedroom, where you can lie down, close your eyes, and breathe for a few moments. It can also be outdoors in the woods or by the ocean, listening to nature's sounds. Or you may be seated on a park bench, in your car, in the lot at work or school. The point is that you need to place yourself in an environment that gives you some time and space to think without distractions running through your mind and then do the grounding exercise you learned before this chapter.

2. **Get into the trance state:** You can do this by breathing and chanting the Om mantra, or if you prefer, you can just sit in silence and allow your conscious mind to dissolve into nothingness as you focus on your breath. While you breathe, keep your intention to connect with your guardian angel front and center in your mind.

3. **Feel their energy:** Once you're in a trance, you'll be able to feel the energy of the angel around you. You may notice some static in the air, a feeling of pressure, an odd coolness or warmth, or even a light caress on your skin. There are other signs your angel may be present, and you'll learn about them in a moment.

4. **Converse with them:** You can tell them anything you want to. You may not get immediate answers, or if you're psychically talented, you may be able to hear back from your angel in real-time. Either way, they have made their presence known to you

means that they're listening to everything you say and will act on your behalf.

5. **Thank them for listening and helping out:** When you're done conversing with your guardian angel, you need to thank them for listening and helping out. The language of gratitude will bring about your success in manifesting the things you want to manifest in your life. Thank them for their constant love and support. If you like, you can ask them to continue to make their presence known and felt in your life.

Remember that there will be times in your life when you won't have time to ground yourself or follow this process to the letter. As long as you make a habit of connecting with your angel, you don't have to worry about following every step. You can just ask them to help you right away, and they'll be off to set things right again.

How to Connect with Other Angels

Sometimes, you may want to connect with other angels known to help with specific things. To connect with them, you have to work with your guardian angel and then ask your guardian angel to put you in touch with the angel you'd like to reach out to. Your angel will come through and honor your request.

Angelic Signs

The following are signs that your angel has heard you or is around you:

You Feel Energized and Happy

If your guardian angel has made their presence known to you and you're connecting with them, you'll often be aware of their presence without even needing to say anything. You'll feel uplifted, inspired, and filled with love from the inside out. Along with feeling so loving toward others, you may find that they are constantly showing you unconditional love.

You See Auras

Many people report seeing angelic auras around them, often describing them as multicolored lights or brighter than normal white auras. The angel's color may differ from yours, but it is generally bright and radiant.

You Feel a Flush or Warmth or Coolness

Your angel may also make their presence known to you in other ways, such as an odd sensation of warmth on your skin or a sudden cool surge of energy through your body. This is the feeling of their energy passing through you.

You Find Feathers around You

These feathers will often be white or a similar color to the angel's aura, and they are the angel's way of leaving a sign for you that they're around. The feathers appear for a reason. Each one is a message from your guardian angel.

You Hear Music

You may also find yourself suddenly hearing beautiful music or singing around you, which can be your angel communicating with you in this way. Their voice will sound unlike anything you've ever heard and can have great healing properties through its frequency.

You Smell an Odd Scent

The most familiar smells around angels are often roses, lavender, or vanilla – but there is no rule about this, and it could be completely different for you. The smell is radiated by your angel to help you recognize them, and it can also give you information about what they're up to at the time.

Chapter 9: Reaching Out to Archangels

Different religions have their own form of angelology as well as rankings of angels. The higher ranks of angels have more authority and power over the ones below them, and the different ranks also look different, with different numbers of faces and wings. The following are the angelic ranks according to the Pseudo-Dionysian work, _Areopagite in De Coelesti Hierarchia_:

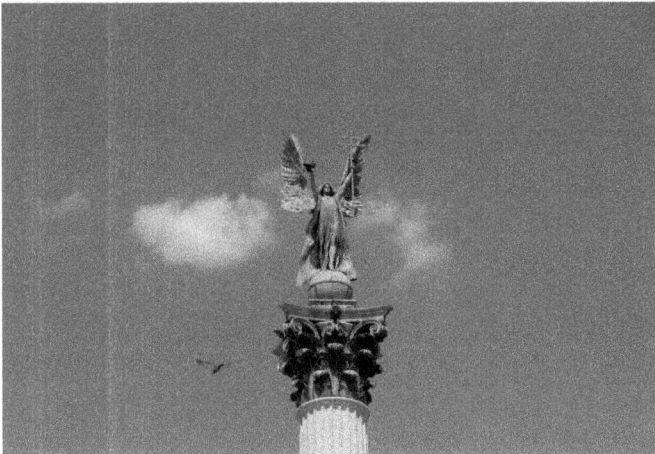

Different religions have their own form of angelology as well as rankings of angels.
https://www.pexels.com/photo/a-bird-flying-near-millennium-monument-under-blue-sky-13717918/

- Seraphim
- Cherubim
- Thrones
- Dominions
- Virtues
- Powers
- Principalities
- Archangels
- Angels

According to Pseudo-Dionysius, the archangels rank higher than angels, but according to the popular consciousness paradigm, archangels are the highest in rank. While the word "archangel" has strong ties to all Abrahamic religions, you can find other beings that resemble them in other traditions and Gnosticism.

The archangels Gabriel and Michael are recognized in Islam, Judaism, and most forms of Christianity. Some Protestants believe that there is only one archangel, Michael. You'll find mention of Raphael in the Book of Tobit, where he is seen as a chief angel, a view also held by the Eastern Orthodox and Catholic churches. Michael, Gabriel, and Raphael are honored by Roman Catholics with special feast days. In Islam, the archangels are Azrael, Israfil, Mikael, and Jibrael. In the Book of Enoch and other Jewish literature, you'll find mention of Metatron, considered above all other angels. However, this angel isn't widely accepted by all.

In some aspects of certain religions, you'll find that there are seven archangels, but their names tend to change depending on whom you ask. The archangels who remain consistent are Michael, Gabriel, and Raphael. The other archangels may vary, but Uriel is acknowledged more often than not and is written about in two Esdras.

Archangels in Zoroastrianism

Many anthropologists, theologists, and philosophers hold that Zoroastrianism is the earliest religious tradition that indicates a belief in the idea of angels. Also known as Mazdaysna, Zoroastrianism holds that there are seven Holy Immortals (or Bounteous Immortals) called the Amesha Spenta. These entities are all rooted in the Ahura Mazda, which is the most powerful of divine beings. These beings are similar to archangels, with immortal bodies that can move through the physical world. They offer guidance, protection, and inspiration to both the spirit and human realms. They are:

- Spenta Mainyu or Spenamino, the Bountiful Spirit
- Asha Vahishta or Ardwahisht, the Highest Truth
- Vohu Mano or Vohuman, the Righteous Mind
- Khshathra Vairya or Shahrewar, the Desirable Dominion
- Spenta Armaiti or Spandarmad, the Holy Devotion
- Haurvatat or Hordad, Perfection or Health
- Ameretat or Amurdad, Immortality

Archangels in Judaism

The Hebrew Bible refers to the archangels as the Elohim. In Hebrew, the word for angel is malakh, meaning "messenger." They are God's very messengers meant to carry out specific tasks. It's not common to find references to these beings in Jewish literature unless you're looking at the later material, like the Book of Daniel. They're talked about briefly in Jacob's stories, and there's mention of Jacob himself having to wrestle with an angel. There's also the story of Lot, who had been given a warning by angels to leave Sodom and Gomorrah. No biblical character referred to angels by name until Daniel. Because of this, it is believed that Jews only became interested in angels while held captive by Babylon. The rabbi Simeon ben Lakish of Tiberias notes that the specific names used by the Jews for angels were gotten from Babylon.

While there weren't any references to archangels in the Hebrew biblical canon, when Rabbinic Judaism superseded Biblical Judaism, there were certain angelic beings who gained prominence and soon had their own personalities, as well as functions they were meant to handle. While these archangels are considered the highest in the hosts of heaven, there was no existing hierarchical system developed. According to Kabbalist and Merkavah mysticism, Metatron rules above them all. Also called Mattatron, he acts as a scribe. He's mentioned in the Talmud and generously written about in the mystical writings of the Merkavah. Michael is seen as Israel's advocate and defender, while Gabriel gets several mentions in the Book of Daniel, the Talmud, and particularly in the Merkavah texts. Here are the twelve archangels according to the Kabbalah, all of them connected to a specific sephira:

1. Metatron
2. Raziel
3. Cassiel
4. Zadkiel
5. Camael
6. Michael
7. Uriel
8. Haniel
9. Raphel
10. Jophiel
11. Gabriel
12. Sandalphon

According to the Book of Enoch, seven holy angels are charged with watching over everyone, and they are considered archangels. They are:

1. Michael
2. Raphael
3. Gabriel
4. Uriel
5. Sariel
6. Raguel
7. Remiel

According to the Apocalypse of Moses or The Life of Adam and Eve, the archangels are:

1. Michael
2. Gabriel
3. Uriel
4. Raphael
5. Joel

Archangels in Christianity

The New Testament of the Bible has more than a hundred references to angelic beings but only refers to archangels in particular twice: once in the First Book of Thessalonians, Chapter 4, verse 16, and again in the Book of Jude, Chapter 1, verse 9. When it comes to the Catholic church, there are three, Gabriel, Michael, and Raphael. Archangels Uriel and Jeremiel are mentioned in four Esdras but aren't considered by the Catholic Church.

Archangels You Can Call On

Michael – the Defender and Protector of All: Michael is the most powerful of the archangels, and he continues to fight against darkness and evil so that the world can have peace. His name means "He who is like God." He often has a pair of scales to measure a soul's weight in divine justice or a sword engulfed in blue flames. His sword and armor represent protection, strength, and courage. He commands the Legion of Light with his sapphire sword in his arm. That sword represents wisdom and discernment, which you can develop the higher you go on the spiritual ladder. His role is to fight evil, protect souls from darkness, help everyone when they die, and see the souls on to their next journey after death. When you call on this archangel, ensure that it's not for something you can easily sort out yourself. You should make sure you're not asking to hurt anyone. If you're invoking Michael for someone else, you should get the person's permission first. This is the archangel to call on in matters of truth, protection, strength, and courage.

Raphael – the Healer: Raphael means "He who heals like God." This is the patron saint of all involved in the art and science of healing the sick and travelers. Raphael is responsible for healing all illnesses of the mind, body, and spirit, and he's a very compassionate being. It doesn't matter what sickness you're dealing with. Turn to him, and he'll help out. He's meant to guide the healers on the earth and is sometimes called "The Medicine of God." He also helps to get rid of demons who have possessed or oppressed people and protects everyone on each trip they take. Reach out to this angel if you want guidance and healing, or have safe travels. Keep in mind that he's more about laughter and the lightness of spirit, no matter how serious things seem. You'll know he's with you when you feel lighter. He has a staff he carries around, with a caduceus. Sometimes he'll show up as a traveler, a pilgrim with a bowl of healing balm and a staff. He's connected to the heart chakra, so when he shows up in visions, you should expect to see emerald green, which is the color of health and nature.

Gabriel — the Messenger: Gabriel is all about getting important messages across to people, so she works closely with journalists, teachers, writers, parents, leaders, and anyone in a position to disseminate information. She has lovely flowing hair of gold and white robes and always carries a trumpet made of polished copper. This angel is also good for creativity, childbirth, child care, and pregnancy. She will also help you in matters of love. Gabriel's name means "The Might of God." Sometimes she's also depicted as a male archangel, holding a lantern in one hand with a lit taper and a green jasper mirror in the other to represent the wisdom of God.

Uriel — the Flame of God: Uriel is the archangel that rules over wisdom and knowledge. According to the Secret Book of John, this is the being in charge of the demons who helped Yaldabaoth, the demiurge, to create Adam, the first human. Usually, this archangel is shown in his cherubic form, also known as the angel of repentance. He was the one who was responsible for looking at the Egyptian doors during the final plague so that those with lamb's blood smeared on the posts would not lose their firstborn sons. This archangel is often shown with a papyrus scroll or a book meant to represent wisdom, and it turns out he's also the patron saint of the arts. Uriel can be seen with a flame in his left hand and a sword in his right. His name means "Light of God."

Sealtiel — the Intercessor of God: Also known as Selaphiel, this angel's name means "Intercessor of God." He is known to play the role of intercessor. For instance, according to the Conflict of Adam and Eve, an apocryphal text of Christianity, this angel was sent along with Suriyel to save Adam and Eve from the serpent's lies. He's also the one who carries the prayers of everyone to the Supreme Being to be answered. According to Eastern Orthodox Christian beliefs, this archangel can help keep children safe, oversee exorcisms, oversee heavenly music, help destroy addictions, and help you interpret your dreams. If you're struggling with feeling cold and unemotional, you can't pay attention, or you continue to get distracted, he's the one to reach out to. He is often seen with his face and eyes turned toward the ground, holding both hands to his bosom as he prays.

Jegudiel — the Glorifier of God: Jegudiel can be seen with a whip with three thongs in his left hand and a wreath of gold in his right hand. His name means "Glorifier of God." He is also called Yadiel, Jadiel, or Jehudiel. Sometimes he holds a crown and the whip to represent the reward you get from the Divine if you're righteous and the punishment you get if you're not. This is the patron saint of those who work, and the crown represents the fruits of one's labors, especially in spiritual terms. He's the one who defends and advises those who work in a position where they have to glorify God, and he's also the one who carries the merciful love of the Source of all life.

Barachiel — the Blessed of God: This archangel carries a white rose, which he holds against his chest. At other times, he shows up with white rose petals all over his cloak, representing the blessings of the Divine raining down on one and all. He could also show up with a staff or a bread basket, representing the blessing of children. The Third Book of Enoch calls him one of the angelic princes, and the Almadel of Solomon calls him one of the chief angels. Barachiel is in charge of all guardian angels, and it is said that everyone must pray to him to get all the good things they desire from their guardian angel. He is the patron saint of married life and family, and he's seen as the one who looks after the children of the Divine.

Jerahmeel — the Exaltation of God: This archangel is responsible for inspiring people to deepen their spiritual practices to connect with the Source of all life. He is responsible for making you think about what you can do to get closer to your Divine Origin. His name means "The Mercy of God." He's also called Remiel or Eremiel, among other names. He looks after those who have passed on as they go along their path in the afterlife. Jerahmeel is also responsible for visions from the Divine, and he's called the archangel of hope.

How to Summon Archangels

Ask your guardian angel to bring them to you: You can summon any archangel you like by asking your guardian angel for their help with that. Summoning archangels can be useful if you want to improve some aspect of your life, whether that's your relationships, physical health, mental health, spiritual journey, and so on.

Say a simple, heartfelt prayer: You can pray to request their presence and assistance in your life. In the past, many have summonsed archangels by using simple prayers said sincerely. Just make sure your intentions are pure and do your best to ensure that you're asking them to come around for something important, not trivial things that you can sort out on your own.

Use their sigils: Another way you can summon the archangels is to work with their sigils. You can get into a state of trance and stare at the sigils while you sit in a meditative state, connecting with their energy and getting their attention. Sigils are magical symbols meant to help connect you with the energy of a specific entity or spirit. You can find the sigils for many archangels on the Internet for free. Simply print them out or draw them on a piece of paper you can gaze at. Here's an angelic sigil ritual you can try out:

1. Draw the sigil on paper to help you connect with the archangel.

2. Put the paper on your altar or on a flat surface.

3. Place three white candles around the sigil and turn off the lights. The candles should be the only source of light in the room.

4. Sit at the table or altar and allow your gaze to fall lightly on the sigil.

5. Breathe deeply and calmly. Note the energy in the room so you can sense any shifts or changes. Also, notice your personal energy.

6. The sigil could become three-dimensional at some point, seeming to rise off the paper. If this happens, do your best to remain calm and unperturbed, so you can keep staring at the sigil.

7. You may visualize the sigil instead of drawing it if you want to. Hold the image in your mind's eye for as long as possible and meditate on it. See it getting brighter and brighter, overpowering the darkness behind your eyelids.

8. When you sense the energy shift, this means the archangel is present. You can make your requests now.

9. Thank them after asking them for whatever you desire, and allow your attention to slowly come back to the room you're in.

Use their name as a mantra: You can invoke the archangel you want by chanting their name as you meditate. You'll need about ten to fifteen minutes. Just repeat the name of the archangel out loud or in your mind. Chanting aloud is good because their names have vibrational frequencies that affect your state of mind and spirit in good ways.

Chapter 10: Cleansing and Defensive Methods

Knowing how to defend yourself spiritually is a good thing, especially if you make a habit of interacting with the spirit realm. This final chapter will tell you everything you need to know about how to cleanse your body and home, protect yourself, and eliminate any unwanted presence or entity from your space or home. Before getting into all that, there's one enemy you have to beware of that could put you in grave danger if you give in to it.

Knowing how to defend yourself spiritually is a good thing, especially if you make a habit of interacting with the spirit realm.
https://www.pexels.com/photo/a-bundle-of-sage-smoking-7947722/

Beware of Fear

The thing about fear is that it is *low-vibration energy* that's very attractive to negative entities. If you go into spirit work with fear in your heart, you'll be a homing beacon for entities that want to cause you trouble or mischief. In fact, calling it *mischief* is putting it lightly because these spirits have been known to make life unbearable for those they latch on to. When you're not afraid of them, you no longer hold any appeal as far as they're concerned, so they have no reason to hang around.

Here are other ways fear can ruin your spirit work:

1. When you fear something new or different, your natural curiosity about the subject disappears. Fear sucks you in and makes you feel like there isn't really anything to be curious about.

2. When you're afraid, you can sometimes stop trusting your instincts. Whatever you are doing, if you don't trust yourself, it's easy to make mistakes or second guess your actions.

3. You can sometimes lose focus on what you are doing when you are afraid and allow your thoughts to run away from you. Scary scenarios start playing in your head, making you jumpy or distracting you from the task.

4. Fear makes it hard for you to hear your guardian angel or other spirits when they need to warn you about something or comfort you. This means that you can find yourself in situations you could have avoided by choosing to remain calm.

What do you do to handle the fear you may feel from doing something new? How do you deal with your nerves when entering uncharted spiritual territory? Sure, you'll have some fearful thoughts, but you need to begin conditioning your mind to ask questions about the phenomena you see. In other words, get curious. It's hard to be curious and afraid at the same time. Think about how you can feel more at home communicating with spirits, what you could do to deepen your relationship with them, how you may make yourself feel safer so you don't feel afraid, and so on. Considering these things and actively working on them will go a long way toward mitigating your fears and worries.

Why Spiritual Cleansing Matters

Spiritual cleansing cannot be overlooked for many reasons. For one thing, it purifies you of any negative or stale energy. Even in your home, sometimes negative energy can intensify, or the energy can get stale from a lack of movement, light, or air in your space. These stagnant, sad energies can cause us much damage in life. You may notice yourself attracting the wrong crowd. You may find that you're suddenly struggling with bills, illness, and other phenomena that aren't normal for you. You may find yourself dealing with nights full of nightmares, unclear messages from your guides, messages from the wrong sorts of spirits, a lack of mental clarity, no peace of mind, and so much more. Besides just getting rid of these energies, spiritual cleansing is good for keeping your aura pure and clean, making it unattractive to harmful spirits. Also, certain deities and other spirits are particular about how you keep your space and body.

How to Cleanse Your Body

There are so many ways you can cleanse your body. You already know how to use salt water, an egg, sage, or a green candle to cleanse yourself. However, it helps to have other methods handy, so you don't feel like you can't cleanse yourself just because you don't have the required tools. Remember that you can cleanse yourself by working with the four classical elements (earth, air, water, and fire) at any time. Let's go over the various options you have:

Smoke Cleansing Rituals: Did you know sage isn't the only thing you can burn to cleanse yourself? You can use the smoke of any woods and herbs besides sage to purify your energy. For instance, you can burn Palo Santo, rabbit tobacco, rose, sweetgrass, lavender, rosemary, cedar, juniper, and so on. It's a good idea to check in with your intuition to see what would suit you best. Otherwise, you may just choose whatever you have available. The idea is to have the smoke touch you everywhere, removing all the negative energies in you.

Spiritual Cleansing Baths: You don't need to use salt when you're doing a spiritual cleansing bath. You can use other things like teas, herbs, crystals, flowers, etc. Some other things to try for your baths are:

- Charge your bath water with crystals. Clear quartz is a good option. You don't have to put the crystal in your bath water. Just let it sit by the tub, and set a clear intention in your mind that you would like to charge the water with cleansing energy through the crystal so that it washes away everything that doesn't belong to you or in you.

- You can charge your bath water with your imagination. Put your hands in the water and shut your eyes. In your mind's eye, see the water as nothing but pure white light. Feel the energy of this water. Notice its purifying power getting stronger and stronger as you move your arms through the water. Say thank you to the water for how it's about to cleanse your body, mind, and spirit, and then have your bath with the water.

- Add mint to your water. Mint is not only cooling but energetically cleansing as well. Adding mint leaves or tea to your bath water is a good way to amplify the cleansing power of your bath. You'll feel refreshed when you've done this.

Fire Cleansing Rituals: Some people like to work with fire to cleanse themselves. Some traditions practice leaping over a fire to cleanse themselves before doing spirit work. Please exercise caution, and don't try this method because you'll probably get hurt or catch on fire if you do. Rather than be this extreme, you can take an unlit candle and roll it over your body. Begin from the top of your head and work your way down to your feet. Imagine the candle absorbing the negative energy from you. Then light the candle so it can expel the negative energy for good.

Crystal Cleansing Rituals: You can use crystal wands of clear quartz or selenite to cleanse yourself. You have to wave the wand around your body and allow it to pick up all the unwanted energy that has stuck to you. When you've finished, you'll need to take the crystal out and bury it in the sand overnight, use sage or some other herb to smudge it, and finally, charge it out in the sunlight or moonlight, so it's ready for the next use. You can also keep your space clean by putting black tourmaline crystals in each room.

Tea Cleansing Rituals: You can drink certain teas to help you cleanse yourself. As an added bonus, the tea will also cleanse you on the inside. Try having kombucha, detox teas, and so on.

Energetic Cleansing Rituals: With this form of ritual, you'll need to be familiar with energy work like reiki. Use the palms of your hands to scan your body for any part that feels energetically blocked. Notice anywhere that has stuck, bad energy. Imagine energy flowing from the palms of your hands to those places. See the energy as white light in your mind's eye. If you can't imagine what it looks like, just feel an intense warmth coming through your palms and cleaning out the parts of you with energetic gunk.

Cleansing Your Sacred Space

It's not enough to cleanse yourself when you're about to communicate with spirits. You have to also think about the space in which you'll be talking to spirits. Your sacred space matters, and you cannot afford to let it accumulate bad energy or vibes. In the same way, your aura can pick up some energetic dirt. The same thing can happen with your home. Every person who has ever set foot in your home has left behind some of their energy. If you were watching something like a true crime documentary or a horror movie, you've affected the energy in your home and made it more attractive to darker energies and entities. If you are feeling sad, down, or angry, that energy lingers unless and until you get rid of it. Even a phone conversation with someone could add energy to your space. The energy of whomever you're talking to can linger. If you've been following so far, it should be pretty obvious that you've got to do something about keeping your space spiritually and energetically clean. You can't just take it for granted that it's clean and continue doing your spiritual work because that's asking for trouble.

Before you do any spirit work in your home or other sacred space, cleanse it. You should do cleansings regularly, every couple of weeks, or every month. This way, you can keep your space safe from bad spirits, vibes, illnesses, strife, and all that other yucky stuff.

Cleansing Your Home with Smudging: You can smudge with any cleansing herb you want. Don't just smudge yourself. Smudge your home, too. You should work from the top to the bottom of the house when smudging. Move from the back to the front. The first thing you've got to do is open up all the doors and windows. This will not only let in more light and air (both elements that have a cleansing vibration), but you'll also make it easier for the negative entities to get out of Dodge. Smudging while keeping the doors and windows closed will accomplish nothing for you.

Another thing to consider when you smudge is you have to address every nook and cranny of your home. Think about those drawers and cupboards you hardly ever open. Open them up and smudge them as well. Think about the corner behind that one door no one ever goes to. Check beneath the beds, the top shelves and cupboards, and so on. You must ensure the negative energy has nowhere to go and fester or hide in your home.

Cleansing Your Home by Asperging: To use this cleansing method, you'll need rue or rosemary. All you need is just a sprig. Dip the herb into blessed water, salt water, or holy water, and then sprinkle the water droplets all over your home as you declare, "I banish all negative energies from this space. Leave now and stay gone."

Cleansing with Floor Washes and Sweeps: A floor wash is meant to help clean the floor of the negative energies it holds onto. You infuse the mop water with herbs that purify your space, or you may sprinkle the herbs on the floor and then use a broom or vacuum cleaner to clean it up. There are many different recipes for making floor washes, but for the most part, they all have about three ingredients added to water. Some recipes require Holy Water or Spiritual Water, and others need Florida Water. However, you can just work with rain water or water from the ocean or a lake, if it's easier for you to get. Whatever you do, you don't want to use tap water, so please stay away from that.

To make your floor wash, you need to put the water you're using into a pot (preferably a non-metal one), add the herbs you prefer, and let them simmer for the next ten minutes. Then take it off the stove and let it cool down before transferring it into a storage container. You're more than welcome if you want to add essential oils to your wash. Just make sure you put them into the storage container first. Don't put them into the boiling hot water. Let the mixture sit for seven days in the sunlight, and then you can use it.

Before using your floor wash, you have to clean the floor as you usually would. Then, you can use the floor wash, beginning from the back of the room and ending at the front door. If there are other floors, work from top to bottom. Pay attention to the house's doorways and give them a good scrub. You can sprinkle some salt at the main entrances to keep away bad energies. The floor wash shouldn't be mopped up when you're done applying it. It's more like a rinse for your regular floor cleaning. So let the floor wash liquid dry on its own, which will activate its power. If you want, adding some of the floor wash liquid to your regular cleaning liquids is okay, which means you'll always be spiritually cleaning your home by default.

What happens if you have wall-to-wall carpets? You can apply the floor wash to the floor by spritzing your carpet or add a bit of the floor wash to your broom and then use that to clean the carpets. You may also consider cleaning your carpets with cleaning liquid, including your floor wash. The following are the ingredients you can add to your floor wash:

- Bay leaves — for healing, purification, and protection.
- Basil — for prosperity.
- Lavender — for tranquility and peace.
- Cedar — for protection and healing.
- Pine needles — for protection.
- Rosemary — for exorcisms, healing, and protection.
- Clove — for eliminating unhappy energy, for protection.
- Juniper — for healing and protection.

Here are some of the essential oils you can add to your floor wash:

- Pine — for prosperity, purification, protection, and healing.
- Dragon's blood — for exorcisms, protection, and purification.
- Patchouli — for prosperity.
- Camphor — for purification.
- Eucalyptus — for healing.
- Cinnamon — for prosperity.
- Lemon grass — for purification.
- Birch — for healing.

Light Cleansing Ritual: Some people enjoy sitting in the dark, even on a nice sunny day, for some reason. If this is you, you need to learn to love the light and begin opening your windows so you can let the light in. The thing about sunlight is that its cleansing ability is extremely powerful. It's so powerful that it sends negative spirits scuttling away for dear life. So make a point of having a home that is bright and full of natural light. Start opening the blinds, and you'll hardly have to worry about negative energy accumulating in your space.

Broom or Besom Cleansing: You can use a special broom (called a besom) to sweep out the bad energy in your space. There are also smaller forms of this broom that you can use to sweep your personal aura from the top of your head to your feet.

Bell Cleansing Ritual: Did you know that sound is an excellent way to cleanse your space and yourself? It's true. You can use certain high-vibration sounds to send negative spirits out of your home. You can play or work with these sounds using chanting, clapping, singing bowls, gongs, bells, and ancient music (think Celtic, Buddhist, and Native American music, Gregorian chants, and so on). These things will keep your space clean and free from unwanted spiritual guests.

Essential Oil Diffusion: You can diffuse essential oils like rosemary, lavender, lemon grass, etc. The smell is another great way to keep your home clean and safe for spirit work.

Making Up Your Own Cleansing Rituals

You can test out all the rituals you've been given to find out what resonates with you the most. For instance, you may prefer an herbal spiritual cleansing bath and then clear out your personal space with sweeping and smudging. It's important to figure out what works best for you so that when you're doing intense spirit work, you know you've covered all your bases, and you don't have to waste time or energy being afraid that the cleansing method you chose isn't quite suitable or enough.

When to Cleanse

You know why cleansing matters. What you may not know is when the right time is to cleanse. Use the following as a guide of sorts:

- Cleanse yourself and your space once a month. Do this preferably during the New Moon or the Waning Moon. You can use an app to find out which phase the moon is in before you do so.

- When you've just recovered from an illness or injury or had to deal with misfortune or death, you should cleanse yourself. Cleanse your home, too.

- When a new season is about to begin, do a cleansing ritual. This will encourage new, vibrant energy full of blessings to flow toward you.

- Before you do any major spirit work, you must cleanse yourself and your home.

- Cleanse yourself after you're done with the spirit work. The same applies to your home.

- Cleanse your home when visitors leave it. Even if the visitors were little babies, cleanse your space.

- Cleanse yourself at least once a week as a form of spiritual maintenance.

- You should do a cleanse whenever you get the sense that you're heavy or your space seems heavy.

- If you're dealing with many emotions, cleanse yourself and your home.

- Whenever a major argument, fight, or misunderstanding occurs, it is important to do a cleanse immediately.

Protection Rituals

Protection rituals are vital for keeping you safe from any negative energy you may be confronted with. Here are some simple and powerful rituals you can do to keep your energy and space protected.

Use Crystals: The best crystals for the job are tourmaline and obsidian, as they're great at absorbing negative energy from their environment. You can create a protection grid with obsidian or black tourmaline. This is the process:

1. Ground yourself first.

2. Take four crystals in both hands and lift them to your Ajna or third eye chakra, which is above your eyes in the middle of both brows on your forehead. In your mind, get clear on your intention for the ritual you're about to do. Then say, "I now program this crystal grid to keep me safe."

3. After this, put the crystals in your home's four corners or cardinal directions. You should have one at the front door, so bad energies can't get in.

Use herbs and salt: The best salt for this is pink Himalayan salt. You can take a bowl of the stuff around your home and sprinkle it everywhere. You can also try the following to incorporate herbs:

1. Get a piece of paper and write "Protection" on it.

2. Put that paper into a fireproof bowl.

3. Put a pinch of salt on the paper, and then drop dill, rosemary, and bay leaves into the bowl. The herbs should be dry.

4. Let your hands hover over the bowl and, in your mind, think about your intention to stay protected.

5. When you're ready, set the contents in the bowl on fire. Please keep a watchful eye on them as they burn.

6. Grind the remnants in the bowl with a mortar and pestle when it's all totally burned. Then put the mixture in your home. This potent ritual will keep your home safe for an entire year.

Full Moon Protection Ritual: You're going to harness the power of the full moon to keep away all negative entities and energies. Here's how it works.

1. Find somewhere you can sit in silence and where you won't be bothered or distracted. You may smudge the place first if you like. Or envision white light or a warm sensation that clears the space.

2. Close your eyes and meditate, keeping your attention on the moonlight.

3. When you're ready, write on paper the stuff you want to eliminate from your life.

4. Read what you've written aloud, and as you do so, see the negative charge behind these things being released to the

universe (or know that it's done if you can't visualize).

5. Take a crystal (obsidian or black tourmaline) and hold it in your left hand. Remain in meditation, contemplating positive energy, until you feel safe and can end the meditation.

Banishing Spirits

Banishing spirits is all about exorcizing them from your space. Sometimes during your spiritual work, some spirits defy you and make themselves at home, slipping through the cracks in your defense. Sometimes, they're there not as a result of your work but because they've been sent to you by someone who doesn't mean you well. Wherever these beings are from, the fact is that you need to get rid of them as soon as possible. Here's what you need to do:

1. Cleanse yourself.

2. Go around your home from top to bottom, back to front, sprinkling salt water or burning sage from one corner to the next. As you do this, say aloud to the spirit, "You're not welcome here, and you were not invited. Leave with immediate effect and never return." You must speak with firmness and do away with fear. You hold power here because they're on your turf and shouldn't be.

3. Next, invoke your ancestors, guardian angel, or any other positive force you want to come into your space. Tell them to take charge and destroy any lingering negative energy in your space. Thank them for helping you out.

Remember, there's no reason to be afraid of interacting with spirits. Ensure you follow the proper procedures, exercise caution, and be ready for anything.

Conclusion

Why is communicating with spirits a wonderful thing? Every time you request something from your spirit guides or speak with deceased loved ones, you open yourself up to the possibility of obtaining amazing gifts, information, and insight. You may also connect with your intuition and gain additional perspective on your life. Speaking with spirit allows you to access higher realms of awareness that can forever change your life.

By communicating with spirits using the information in this book, you will notice a big difference in both the vividness and clarity of your dreams and the ability to project yourself into a higher realm of consciousness that transcends time and space. This is a very powerful meditation that can be used on its own or with any other psychic development or spirit communication practice. You'll also begin experiencing many "coincidences," which are really synchronicity. Your life will be more aligned, and things will begin to flow much easier for you. You'll experience this because humans aren't just physical but spiritual. This means the process of meditation and connecting with the spirit realm leads to your spiritual nourishment, so you live a more balanced life in this world and the one beyond.

If you have ever wanted to communicate with spirits but haven't found the comfort level yet, this book should help you reach that point. It's said that until you establish communication with your spirits and guide, you are only using 10% of your potential. Communicating with spirits will benefit you greatly in every aspect of your life by opening up and allowing yourself to grow spiritually. To be a great communicator, you must take the first step. This is where this book will come in handy. It will guide you in receiving the amazing gifts spirits have for you. Anyone can learn how to communicate with spirits once they know how it's done and what it involves.

Sadly, more people don't speak with their loved ones and spirits. They pretend that they don't believe in anything that doesn't involve an afterlife, body, or brain when communicating with the spirit world is very real. You can have conversations with them just like you can have a conversation with a friend who's still on this side of life with you. The ability to communicate with spirits is a gift that people don't use often enough, sadly. The only thing you need to do to be a successful communicator is to be willing and open. When you start, you'll be incredibly shocked that it took you this long to open yourself up to the spirit realm, and you won't want to live any other way.

Your life is not only about you. It's also about everyone else who has gone before. You can learn a lot from those who have passed on. Most of the time, this information is given to you for your own good. Communicating with a spirit can give you answers to questions that will forever change your perspective on life. It takes courage to step out of your comfort zone, but it's well worth it if you are open and willing to learn new things.

You should give this book another read, taking notes the second time. This way, you can ensure that you're ready for the journey ahead. Spirits have a lot to share with us, and entering the spirit realm is worthwhile. So many wonderful gifts may be given to you, so don't miss out. Be ready for the wonder of spirit communication with this book.

Here's another book by Mari Silva that you might like

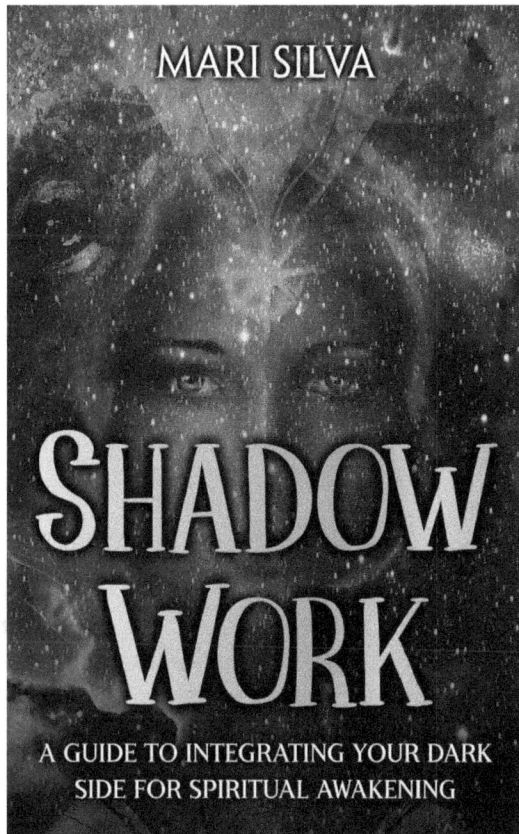

Your Free Gift
(only available for a limited time)

Thanks for getting this book! If you want to learn more about various spirituality topics, then join Mari Silva's community and get a free guided meditation MP3 for awakening your third eye. This guided meditation mp3 is designed to open and strengthen ones third eye so you can experience a higher state of consciousness. Simply visit the link below the image to get started.

https://spiritualityspot.com/meditation

References

Anthony, M. (2015). Evidence of Eternity: Communicating with Spirits for Proof of the Afterlife. Llewellyn Worldwide.

Berkowitz, R. S., & Romaine, D. S. (2002). The Complete Idiot's Guide to Communicating with Spirits. Penguin.

bor Klaniczay, G. (Ed.). (2005). Communicating with the Spirits (Vol. 1). Central European University Press.

Buckland, R. (2005). The spirit book: The encyclopedia of clairvoyance, channeling, and spirit communication. Visible Ink Press.

Hunter, J. (2011). Talking with the spirits: Anthropology and interpreting spirit communication. Journal of the Society for Psychical Research.

Leclere, A. (2005). Seeing the Dead, Talking with Spirits: Shamanic Healing through Contact with the Spirit World. Simon and Schuster.

Leonard, T. J. (2005). Talking to the other side: a history of modern spiritualism and mediumship: a study of the religion, science, philosophy, and mediums that encompass this American-made religion. iUniverse.

McMullin, S. E. (2004). Anatomy of a Seance: A History of Spirit Communication in Central Canada. McGill-Queen's Press-MQUP.

Hunter, J. (2010). Talking with the Spirits: More than A Social Reality?. Paranormal Review.

Virtue, D. (1997). Angel Therapy: Healing messages for every area of your life. Hay House, Inc.

Virtue, D. (2010). Archangels and Ascended Masters. ReadHowYouWant. com.

Virtue, D. (2002). Earth Angels. Hay House, Inc.

Virtue, D. (1999). Healing with the Angels. Hay House, Inc.